Effective Business Plans
A Step-by-Step Guide

Charlton Hall, PhD

Charlton Hall, PhD

Elder Grove Media

www.eldergrovemedia.com

ISBN: 9798871058312

Charlton Hall, PhD

CONTENTS

Charlton Hall, PhD

1 Why Write a Business Plan?

In the dynamic and often unpredictable world of entrepreneurship, the significance of a well-crafted business plan cannot be overstated. It serves as the North Star, guiding entrepreneurs through the intricacies of launching, managing, and growing a successful venture.

While it can always be tempting to dive headfirst into the entrepreneurial arena, the wisdom of developing a comprehensive business plan lies in its ability to provide structure, foster strategic thinking, attract stakeholders, and ultimately pave the way for sustained success. In this book we will delve into the multifaceted importance of having a good business plan for your venture. In this chapter we will be exploring how this foundational document serves as the bedrock and the guidepost for entrepreneurial success.

To be truly successful and thrive in your business, a well-thought out and well-written business plan is a necessity. Such a document becomes your entity's "bible," dictating how and when strategic business decisions are made.

Clarity of Vision and Mission

At the heart of any successful business lies a clear and compelling vision. This vision is a guiding light that illuminates the path forward. A well-structured business plan serves as the canvas on which entrepreneurs paint the picture of their vision and mission. By meticulously articulating the purpose and direction of the venture, the business plan not only aligns the internal compass of the entrepreneur but also communicates a coherent narrative to potential stakeholders, employees, and investors.

The process of creating a business plan compels entrepreneurs to reflect deeply on the core purpose of their venture. What problem does the business aim to solve? What value does it bring to the market? Why is my business different from all the other similar ones out there? What added value am I bringing to the market?

These fundamental questions, when answered within the confines of a business plan, lay the foundation for a business rooted in a clear and distinct purpose.

A business plan ensures that every aspect of the venture aligns harmoniously with its overarching goals. This alignment is crucial for maintaining a unified front among team members and stakeholders. Whether it's the marketing strategy, operational processes, or financial objectives, the business plan acts as a guiding force, ensuring that all efforts are directed toward the realization of the established goals.

Beyond its internal functions, a well-crafted business plan also becomes a powerful communication tool. It offers a succinct and organized way to convey the vision and mission of the business to internal and external audiences. This clarity of communication fosters understanding, aligns expectations, and cultivates a shared sense of purpose among all stakeholders.

Strategic Planning and Decision-Making

The intricacies of the business environment demand a strategic approach to planning and decision-making. A business plan acts as a compass, providing entrepreneurs with the necessary tools to navigate the complexities of the market, competition, and operational challenges.

A well-written business plan can assist in strategic planning and decision-making in the following areas:

A. Market Analysis

One of the primary functions of a business plan is to conduct a comprehensive analysis of the market. This involves understanding the target audience, evaluating industry trends, and assessing the competitive landscape. Through this process, entrepreneurs gain valuable insights that inform strategic decisions and help position the business effectively within the market.

B. Risk Assessment

Every business venture comes with inherent risks. From economic uncertainties to unforeseen challenges, entrepreneurs must be equipped to identify, assess, and mitigate risks. A good business plan serves as a risk management tool, providing a structured framework for recognizing potential pitfalls and developing proactive strategies to navigate them.

C. Resource Allocation

Efficient resource allocation is a cornerstone of any business or any successful entrepreneurship. A business plan aids in the strategic allocation of resources, be it financial, human, or technological. By outlining priorities and delineating resource needs, entrepreneurs can maximize the impact of their investments and ensure a judicious use of available resources.

D. Setting Realistic Expectations

Business owners are naturally excited about their ventures, but they shouldn't allow their excitement to lead them to over-promise what they can do. In the fervor of entrepreneurship, setting realistic expectations is often a delicate balancing act. A business plan compels entrepreneurs to establish achievable milestones and goals. These benchmarks serve as yardsticks for measuring success, providing a realistic framework that guides the entrepreneur and the team through the journey of building a viable business.

Operational Efficiency and Organization

The internal workings of a business demand a well-organized and efficient operational framework. A business plan acts as a blueprint for structuring the organization, streamlining processes, and preparing for unforeseen circumstances. Some ways an effective business plan can lead to organization and operational efficiency include:

A. Establishing Structure

Organizational structure is a critical aspect of operational efficiency. A business plan outlines the hierarchy, roles, and responsibilities within the organization, providing clarity on reporting lines and ensuring that every team member understands their role in achieving the business's objectives.

B. Streamlining Processes

Efficiency in operational processes is directly correlated with a business's ability to deliver products or services effectively. A business plan prompts entrepreneurs to identify and optimize key processes, eliminating redundancies and bottlenecks. This streamlining enhances overall efficiency and contributes to the seamless functioning of the business.

C. Contingency Planning

In the unpredictable world of business, the ability to adapt to unforeseen circumstances is paramount. A well-constructed business plan includes contingency plans that prepare the business to navigate challenges and disruptions effectively. Whether it is changes in the market, unexpected economic downturns, or internal challenges, a business plan equips entrepreneurs with strategies to weather the storms.

Financial Viability and Sustainability

Financial viability and sustainability are at the core of every business venture. This area is what most people think of when they think of effective business plans, and writing this section of your business plan well is key to attracting investors, as this is usually the first section an investor turns to after reading the Executive Summary. A good business plan provides a roadmap for financial success by offering realistic projections, attracting funding, and ensuring long-term sustainability.

Some key areas to consider include:

A. Financial Projections

Financial projections are an integral component of any business plan. Entrepreneurs must forecast revenue, expenses, and profits over a defined period. These projections serve not only as a guide for financial decision-making but also as a tool for attracting investors and lenders.

B. Funding and Investment

For many ventures, securing external funding is a critical step in realizing their vision. A well-prepared business plan is often the first document investors and lenders review. It provides them with a comprehensive understanding of the business model, revenue potential, and the entity's strategy for utilizing funds effectively.

C. Long-Term Sustainability

Beyond the initial phases of a business, sustainability is a key consideration. A well-written business plan helps entrepreneurs envision the long-term trajectory of their venture. By assessing market trends, planning for growth, and adapting to changing landscapes, entrepreneurs can position their businesses for sustained success.

Investor and Stakeholder Confidence

The confidence investors and stakeholders have in your venture is instrumental in the growth and development of a business. A well-thought-out business plan plays a pivotal role in instilling this confidence by reflecting professionalism, credibility, and a clear path to success.

Some key areas to consider when hoping to instill investor and stakeholder confidence in your entity include:

A. Professionalism and Credibility

If you can't take your business seriously, investors and other stakeholders won't take you seriously. Investors and stakeholders seek assurance that their investments will yield returns. A meticulously crafted business plan not only showcases the entrepreneur's dedication and professionalism but also communicates a level of credibility that instills confidence in those considering involvement with the venture.

B. Transparency

Open and transparent communication is essential for building trust. A business plan provides a transparent overview of the entity's goals, strategies, and financial projections. This transparency fosters trust among investors and stakeholders, creating a solid foundation for collaboration and support.

Scalability

Scalability is a key consideration for businesses aiming for growth. Scalability is about building a business that can grow efficiently and sustainably. It requires careful planning, strategic decision-making, and a business model that can adapt to changing circumstances.

By addressing scalability in the business plan, investors and stakeholders gain confidence that the organization is well-prepared for growth and capable of maximizing opportunities without compromising its core operations or financial health.

Scalability in an effective business plan refers to the ability of a business to handle increased demands, expand its operations, and grow without a proportional increase in costs or a significant decrease in efficiency. A scalable business is one that can adapt and accommodate growth without encountering substantial obstacles or requiring a complete overhaul of its structure, processes, or systems.

When discussing scalability in the context of a business plan, several key elements should be considered:

Operational Scalability

This aspect focuses on the business's capacity to handle a larger volume of transactions, customers, or activities without a linear increase in resources or costs. Efficient operational scalability ensures that the business can grow seamlessly without encountering bottlenecks or diminishing the quality of its products or services.

Financial Scalability

Financial scalability pertains to the ability of a business to grow revenue and profits without incurring a proportional increase in expenses. A financially scalable business model allows for sustainable growth, as increased sales or market share doesn't lead to a direct rise in operational or production costs.

Technological Scalability

In our technology-driven world, businesses must ensure that their systems and infrastructure can scale to accommodate growing demands. This includes the scalability of IT systems, software, and hardware to handle increased user loads or expanded functionalities.

Human Resources Scalability

A business plan should address how the organization intends to scale its workforce to meet the demands of growth. This involves considerations such as hiring plans, training programs, and the ability to attract and retain talent as the business expands.

Product or Service Scalability

The scalability of a business's offerings is crucial. A scalable product or service can meet the needs of a growing customer base without significant modifications or a decrease in quality. This may involve developing products with broad market appeal or ensuring that services can be efficiently delivered at scale. This may include increasing supply chain capacity, acquiring new resources, or hiring more staff.

Market Scalability

A scalable business plan considers the scalability of the target market. It assesses whether the products or services can meet the demands of a larger audience or if expansion into new markets is feasible without fundamental changes to the business model.

Financial Model Scalability

The financial model presented in the business plan should demonstrate how the business can achieve profitability and sustainability as it scales. This includes forecasting revenue growth, cost structures, and profit margins over different stages of expansion. This may require extensive market research and projections based on existing market data.

Risk Management and Scalability

Scalability also involves anticipating and mitigating risks associated with growth. A well-prepared business plan addresses potential challenges that may arise during expansion and outlines strategies to manage and minimize these risks.

Guiding Growth and Expansion

The journey of any successful business venture involves phases of growth and expansion. A well-structured business plan guides entrepreneurs through the complexities of scaling their ventures, ensuring that growth is strategic, sustainable, and aligned with the overall vision.

When you take the time to write an effective business plan you are telling your investors and stakeholders that you are a competent and organized professional worthy of their investment in your business.

2 The Executive Summary

The executive summary stands as a critical component to a successful business plan. It is an encapsulation of the entire plan that beckons readers to delve deeper. As the gateway to understanding the essence of a business venture, a well-crafted executive summary not only grabs attention but also serves as a persuasive tool for investors, stakeholders, and potential partners.

Think of it as your "elevator speech" about your business. A well-written executive summary should be a quick overview of your business so that a person who doesn't have time to read the whole plan will still have a good idea of what your business is about.

Additionally, a good Executive Summary should encourage the reader to want to delve more deeply into the rest of the plan to learn more about your business.

Concise clarity is the essence of an excellent Executive Summary. To achieve this concise clarity, a good Executive Summary should start by summarizing the business plan's key points, ensuring clarity and simplicity in language for easy comprehension from a wide variety of readers with differing educational backgrounds.

Remember when writing this section especially to use engaging language designed to capture the reader's attention. this will be the first section your audience will read, so it could be compelling enough to encourage them to read further. To achieve this, try employing engaging and persuasive language by capturing the reader's attention and creating interest. Put yourself in their shoes. If you were an investor or loan officer, what would you be looking for when reading a business plan? What sorts of things would you be looking for that would capture your attention if you were doing their job? Once you figure that out, put it in your Executive Summary.

One way to do this is by using a visionary tone that conveys enthusiasm for the business and talks about your vision for the future. If you're focused on long-term strategies and financial growth, you have a much better chance of inspiring confidence in the business's potential for success.

COMPANY CORE VALUES

Your Executive Summary should begin with your venture's core message. This is the "take home" you want readers to know about your business. What does your company value? What is its reason for existing? What makes you unique from other businesses? What can you offer a potential client that no other company can provide? If you have mission and vision statements, this would be a good place to include them. In fact, many Executive Summaries open with a mission statement followed by a vision statement.

OVERVIEW OF THE BUSINESS

Next comes the Overview of the Business section. If you haven't already included these in the previous section, then go ahead and list your company's mission and vision statements here. Once you've included your mission and vision statements, you may want to explain their significance for the reader. Here is where you provide context for the reader to understand the business's purpose.

MARKET OPPORTUNITY

This section should include a Market Opportunity statement identifying the market gap or opportunity the business seeks to address. In this section, usually no more than a paragraph or two, explain what makes your business unique and why it is exceptionally qualified to meet the market opportunity addressed by your business. Present a clear picture of the target market and its potential. State in clear, concise, and precise language why your business is uniquely suited to exploit this particular market.

Next comes your venture's Business Model. This section outlines the fundamental structure of how the business operates, describing revenue streams, pricing strategies, and key partnerships. Are you a sole proprietorship, a partnership, a Limited Liability Corporation, a non-profit, an S Corporation, a C Corporation, or some other type of entity?

FINANCIAL SNAPSHOT

Now we come to the Financial Snapshot. This critical section of your Business plan exists to paint a portrait of the financial viability of your business. If yours is a business that already exists, highlight some of your previous financial achievements. Examples to include in this section might be:

- Increased revenue by 10%
- Achieved a net profit margin of 15%
- Reduced operating expenses by 5%
- Improved cash flow management
- Maintained a positive cash flow
- Increased market share by 5%
- Achieved a return on investment (ROI) of 20%
- Reduced debt by 10%

This section is critical if you intend to use your business plan for fundraising like getting loans, grants, or other types of investors. Investors may or may not have a particular interest in the goods or services your company provides. Generally they're mainly concerned with profit vs. loss. What is their likely return on investment? How safe is their money if they invest it in you, and what sort of return on investment (ROI) can they reasonably expect?

This is the section for presenting key financial metrics and projections. Your goal here is to demonstrate
the business's financial viability and potential for growth.

You will also include your entity's funding requirements in this section. Here is where you clearly state the financial resources required for the business. Make sure to specify how the funds will be allocated to support growth and expansion of the business.

TEAM SHOWCASE

For a pre-existing business, the Team Showcase section is where you get to brag about your staff. Start off with your Leadership Team by introducing its key members and showcasing their relevant experience and expertise. What makes your staff unique from every other similar business in the field? What accomplishments set your staff apart?

Next is the Key Roles and Responsibilities for each member of the staff. When writing this section, focus on outlining the roles and responsibilities of key team members, illustrating how the team's skills align with the business's goals.

CALL TO ACTION

Every Business Plan is written for a purpose. That purpose is to elicit some sort of action from your audience. In the Call to Action section of your business plan, you are encouraging further exploration by asking your audience to read further. You can do this by closing the executive summary with a call to action.

If you have done a good job of writing your Executive Summary, you have encouraged readers to explore the business plan in more depth for a deeper understanding.

The executive summary serves as the gateway to your business plan, encapsulating its essence and inviting readers to explore your entity further. Crafting a compelling executive summary requires a delicate balance of conciseness, clarity, and engagement. When executed effectively, it transforms a mere introduction into a persuasive narrative that captivates stakeholders and sets the stage for a deeper understanding of the business plan. As the first impression of a business venture, a well-written executive summary is a powerful tool that can pave the way for success.

3 Industry Overview

When crafting a business plan, one of the foundational elements that demands meticulous attention is the Industry Overview. This section serves as the gateway to understanding the broader landscape in which a business operates, providing valuable insights for entrepreneurs, investors, and stakeholders alike. In this chapter, we will delve into the significance of the Industry Overview within a business plan, the key components it should encompass, and the strategic insights it offers for steering a business toward success.

At its core, the Industry Overview is a comprehensive examination of the industry or market in which a business intends to operate. It serves as the backdrop against which the entity's strategies, opportunities, and challenges unfold. The primary objective of this section is to offer a contextual understanding of the industry's current state, trends, and dynamics.

Components of an Effective Industry Overview

Certain elements are an absolute necessity when writing an effective Industry Overview for your business plan. When this section is well-written, it lets your investors and stakeholders know that you are a professional organization.

Some of the key elements to include in your Industry Overview are:

1. Market Definition and Segmentation

Your Industry Overview should clearly define the boundaries of the market in which the business operates. Segment the market based on relevant criteria such as demographics, geography, or product categories.

2. Market Size and Growth

Provide data on the current size of the market and its historical growth patterns. Project future market growth based on trends and emerging opportunities. This, like other sections of your business plan, will require some research on your part. A good place to start with research is your local Chamber of Commerce or Small Business Administration. You might also check the Small Business Administration's website at https://www.sba.gov.

3. Industry Trends and Drivers

Identify and analyze prevailing trends influencing your particular industry. Highlight the key drivers shaping the market's direction.

4. Competitive Landscape

Conduct a thorough analysis of existing competitors. Assess the strengths, weaknesses, opportunities, and threats (SWOT) of key players. Identify market leaders, disruptors, and potential collaborators. When writing this section, don't forget to differentiate your entity from others in the market. Why should investors and stakeholders go with your business and not some other? What do you do differently that would make your business a success in a competitive market?

5. Regulatory Environment

Explore the regulatory landscape governing the industry. Highlight any legal or compliance considerations that may impact business operations. Be aware of any safety regulations or permits or licenses needed for your chosen industry.

6. Customer Behavior and Preferences

Understand the behaviors, needs, and preferences of target customers. Analyze purchasing patterns and factors influencing buying decisions, and use these to your advantage in your marketing strategy.

7. Barriers to Entry

Identify entry barriers that new businesses may face. Are you an existing business or are you starting from scratch? What will your entity bring to the market that isn't already available elsewhere? Assess the level of competition and potential challenges for market newcomers.

8. Supplier and Vendor Dynamics

Examine the relationships between businesses and their suppliers or vendors in your chosen market. Evaluate the potential impact of supplier dynamics on the business's operations. Are there any potential supply chain shortages that could impact your business? What will you do if this occurs? What about the labor market? This is a critical area if you are a service-based entity that relies on human capital, especially if there is a shortage of skilled labor in your industry.

Are there enough vendors to meet supply and demand for your chosen venture? Don't forget to include shipping costs. Are your raw materials available locally, or will they have to be transported over great distances? Can you obtain resources from multiple vendors, or are you relying solely on one or two vendors? If those vendors go out of business, how will it impact your own organization?

9. Technology and Innovation

Explore the role of technology in your chosen industry. Highlight areas of innovation and potential technological disruptions. If the technological landscape changes, how might such change impact your entity? A recent example to examine would be the impact of Artificial Intelligence (AI) on creative ventures like graphic design, music composition, and video editing. Technology changes rapidly, and an effective business plan will reflect current awareness of technological trends.

10. Economic Factors

Consider broader economic factors influencing the industry, such as GDP trends, inflation, or unemployment rates. Evaluate the industry's sensitivity to economic fluctuations, and your particular venture's capability of handling and adapting to such economic fluctuations.

Strategic Insights Derived from the Industry Overview

The purpose of an Industry Overview is to analyze the current market and your business entity's role in it. When investors and stakeholders review your business plan they will be looking for certain information that can give them insights into your business venture. Some of these insights include:

1. Risk Mitigation

Any business venture contains an element of risk. Investors will be looking at your business plan for risk management strategies. Understanding the industry landscape for your chosen market allows you to proactively identify and mitigate potential risks.

By assessing regulatory, economic, or competitive risks, your business can develop strategies to navigate uncertainties effectively.

2. Opportunity Recognition

An in-depth industry overview reveals untapped opportunities. Recognizing emerging trends or market gaps enables a business to position itself strategically to capitalize on these opportunities. Pay particular attention to opportunities specific to your type of business.

3. Competitive Strategy Formulation

Armed with insights from the competitive landscape, businesses can formulate robust strategies. This is why a well-researched and well-written Industry Overview is critical to your venture. Whether through differentiation, cost leadership, or niche targeting, understanding your competition is fundamental to gaining a competitive edge.

4. Resource Allocation

The Industry Overview aids in efficient resource allocation. Businesses can align their budgets and investments with the prevailing market conditions and opportunities, ensuring optimal use of resources. Remember to focus on the unique resource needs of your chosen market and your chosen business.

5. Market Positioning

Understanding customer behaviors and preferences facilitates effective market positioning. Businesses can tailor their products, services, and marketing strategies to align with what resonates most with their target audience. This means that you will have to know your target demographic. What sort of customer will purchase your goods or services? What attracts them to your business and not one of your competitors? What unique market niche will your venture fill?

6. Informed Decision-Making

Strategic decisions, from product development to expansion plans, are best made in the context of industry dynamics. The Industry Overview equips decision-makers with the information needed to make informed and calculated choices.

7. Adaptability and Innovation

Recognizing technological trends and innovations within the industry allows businesses to stay ahead of the curve. The ability to adapt and innovate is crucial for long-term success and relevance.

A well-written and effective Industry Overview section considers as many potential market changes as possible and has contingency plans for all of those anticipated situations.

While it is probably impossible to predict all potential risks, including as many as possible and your plan for dealing with them should they arise will demonstrate to your investors and stakeholders that you are an organized professional.

Stakeholder Confidence

An insightful Industry Overview instills confidence in investors, partners, and stakeholders. It demonstrates that the business is not operating in isolation but is deeply aware of its external environment. When you write an effective Industry Overview you are letting your potential investors know that you are a serious, professional entrepreneur worth their time and investment.

Crafting an Industry Overview: Best Practices

When you prepare to write the Industry Overview section of your business plan, there are certain practices that need to be considered. This is true whether you are writing it yourself or whether you have contracted for it to be written. In the latter case, when reviewing business plans that others have written you should consider these components when evaluating their work.

These elements are:

Thorough Research

The Industry Overview is not just a perfunctory section within a business plan. It is the cornerstone upon which strategic decisions are built. An effective Industry Overview empowers businesses to navigate the complexities of their external environment, turning challenges into opportunities and uncertainties into strategic advantages.

When you craft a business plan, dedicating the necessary time and resources to the Industry Overview is an investment in understanding, preparation, and ultimately, success.

You should conduct extensive industry research using a combination of primary and secondary sources. Leverage industry reports, market analyses, and interviews with industry experts.

Ensure that data presented in the Industry Overview is accurate, up-to-date, and verifiable. Cross-reference information from multiple sources where possible to enhance reliability.

Communicate complex information in a clear and concise manner. Use visuals where needed such as charts or graphs to enhance clarity.

Consider the knowledge level of the target audience, and write this section accordingly. While many investors have extensive knowledge of the business landscape, they may know little about your particular industry. Write your Industry Overview as if you are talking to someone who knows nothing about your particular industry. Tailor the Industry Overview to meet the needs of both industry experts and those less familiar with the market.

Data Accuracy

Nothing can make or break a business more quickly than presenting erroneous information in your business plan. At best it demonstrates a lack of professionalism. At worst, it could be interpreted by investors and other stakeholders as a deliberate attempt to deceive them as to the status of your business in relation to others in your industry's market.

Ensure that data presented in the Industry Overview is accurate, up-to-date, and verifiable. Cross-reference information from multiple sources to enhance reliability whenever possible.

Clear Presentation

In some types of business entity, especially those in scientific or technical markets, there can be a lot of jargon that is specific to the market. Be aware of this and communicate complex information in a clear and concise manner. Use visuals such as illustrations, charts or graphs to enhance clarity.

Consider the knowledge level of the target audience. Tailor the Industry Overview section to meet the needs of both industry experts and those less familiar with the market.

Continuous Updates

Recognize that industry landscapes constantly evolve. Commit to regularly updating the Industry Overview to reflect the latest trends, market shifts, and emerging factors. A good rule of thumb is to update this section on a quarterly basis at a minimum.

The Industry Overview is not just a perfunctory section within a business plan, It is the cornerstone upon which strategic decisions are built. An effective Industry Overview empowers businesses to navigate the complexities of their external environment, turning challenges into opportunities and uncertainties into strategic advantages.

Dedicating the necessary time and resources to the Industry Overview is an investment in understanding, preparation, and ultimately, success in a competitive business landscape.

4 Products or Services Offered

The Products or Services Offered section of your business plan delineates the essence of what a business brings to the market. This section is not merely a list of offerings but should also include a strategic narrative that communicates the value proposition, uniqueness, and market positioning of a business's products or services.

In this chapter we will explore the key components and strategies for writing an effective Products or Services Offered section that captivates stakeholders and sets the stage for business success.

Strategic Significance of the Products or Services Offered Section

At its core, the Products or Services Offered section is more than a catalogue of what a business sells. It is a narrative that articulates the fundamental value proposition to customers, delineates differentiation from competitors, and outlines how the offerings meet the needs of the target market.

This section is the linchpin that connects the internal workings of the business with the external demands of the market. Some essential components of the Products or Services Offered section should always include:

1. Clear Description of Offerings

Begin with a concise and clear description of the products or services. Define the core features and functionalities that distinguish them in the market. Focus on why your products or services are unique and why a potential customer (or investor) should chose your product over all the other available products in the market.

2. Unique Selling Proposition (USP)

Investors and potential customers want to know how your products or services are different. Clearly articulate the unique selling proposition or competitive advantage of the offerings your company can produce.

Highlight what sets your products or services apart from alternatives in the market.

3. Value Proposition

Explicitly state the value the offerings bring to customers. This is not just their cost or price. Identify the problems or needs they address and the benefits they deliver.

The goal is to create a competitive advantage by offering products or services with higher perceived value than those of your competitors.

When done effectively, this can lead to customer loyalty, positive word-of-mouth, and increased market share. Understanding and effectively delivering value-added propositions are essential components of successful business planning and execution.

4. Target Market Relevance

When reviewing the products or services offered by your entity, link the products or services to the needs and preferences of the target market. Be sure to link these needs and preferences to your particular products or services using the research you did in the previous Industry Overview section of your business plan.

Demonstrate an understanding of customer demographics, behaviors, and pain points using verifiable, measurable data.

In the context of business, a *pain point* refers to a specific problem, challenge, or frustration that potential customers are experiencing and that a business aims to address.

Identifying and understanding these pain points is crucial for your business to tailor your products, services, or solutions to meet the needs and alleviate the challenges your target audience face.

5. Product Lifecycle

A product's life cycle is the stages a product goes through from its introduction to the market until its eventual withdrawal or discontinuation.

The product life cycle is a crucial framework for businesses to understand the dynamics of a product's market performance and make informed decisions regarding marketing, production, and strategic planning.

The typical product life cycle consists of four stages: *introduction, growth, maturity,* and *decline* (see *Appendices* for further information).

If applicable, discuss where the offerings stand in their lifecycle. Outline plans for product development, enhancement, or diversification with an eye towards what market research says about these factors.

6. Intellectual Property

If relevant, discuss any intellectual property associated with your entity's offerings. Highlight patents, trademarks, copyrights, or proprietary technologies that contribute to your company's uniqueness.

7. Scalability and Adaptability

Although scalability and adaptability should have been addressed in the Industry Overview section, in the Products and Services Offered section you will use the data from the Industry Overview section to describe how scalability and adaptability relate specifically to the products and/or services your entity offers.

Address the scalability of products or services to meet growing demand, using market data previously discussed in the Industry Overview section. If necessary, include research specific to your products or services in this section.

Discuss how offerings can adapt to changing market conditions or emerging trends. Be sure to include the data you researched about how market conditions will impact the scalability and adaptability of your products and services.

8. Pricing Strategy

Provide insight into the pricing strategy for the offerings. Explain the rationale behind pricing decisions and how it aligns with the perceived value.

A well-defined pricing strategy takes into account various factors, including production costs, market demand, competitor pricing, and perceived customer value.

Businesses can adopt different pricing models, such as cost-plus pricing, value-based pricing, penetration pricing, or skimming pricing, depending on their market positioning and goals.

The chosen pricing strategy plays a crucial role in influencing consumer behavior, brand perception, and overall profitability. Striking the right balance between offering competitive prices and capturing the perceived value of the product or service is essential for long-term success.

The pricing strategy should align with the overall business strategy, considering factors like market positioning, target customer segments, and the company's broader financial objectives.

Effective pricing strategies not only contribute to revenue generation but also impact brand perception and market competitiveness.

9. Distribution Channels

Describe the channels through which the offerings will reach customers. Distribution channels are the pathways through which businesses get their products or services into the hands of customers. Distribution channels encompass the various intermediaries and methods used to move goods or services from production to consumption.

These channels can range from direct sales to consumers through company-owned stores or online platforms to indirect methods involving wholesalers, retailers, agents, and other intermediaries.

The choice of distribution channels depends on factors such as product type, target market, geographical reach, and the overall business strategy. Efficient distribution channels play a pivotal role in ensuring products are available where and when customers need them, optimizing accessibility and convenience.

Striking the right balance in channel selection, management, and coordination is imperative for businesses seeking to maximize market penetration, enhance customer satisfaction, and ultimately achieve sustainable growth in a competitive marketplace.

When writing this section, outline distribution strategies, partnerships, or collaborations that enhance accessibility.

10. Regulatory Compliance

If applicable, discuss any regulatory compliance requirements associated with your offerings. Address how your business ensures adherence to any applicable industry standards and regulations.

Ensure that anyone, regardless of their familiarity with the industry, can understand how your offerings comply with any established regulations.

Demonstrating Strategic Thinking

The Products or Services Offered section is not just a static description of your commodities. It is a testament to the strategic thinking of the business. It showcases the alignment of offerings with market needs, the foresight in planning for scalability, and the agility to adapt to evolving circumstances. An effective Products and Services Offered section not only informs but inspires confidence in stakeholders, conveying that the business is not merely selling products or services but delivering a solution that adds genuine value to the market.

The Products or Services Offered section is the focal point that radiates the essence of the business. Crafting this section demands a fusion of strategic clarity, effective communication, and an intimate understanding of the market landscape. This section should be the narrative thread that weaves the business's story into the fabric of the market, setting the stage for success.

5 Market Analysis

The Market Analysis section of a business plan guides investors, stakeholders, and potential customers through the dynamic terrain of your industry's target market. It provides a comprehensive understanding of the industry, the market, customers, competitors, and potential challenges and opportunities for your business entity.

The components to understanding the Market Analysis include:

1. Define the Scope of the Market
Begin the Market Analysis section of your business plan by clearly defining the industry and market segment your business operates within. Specify geographical boundaries, target demographics, and any relevant product or service categories. Will you be selling limited to a particular geographical location? What market factors will impact that decision? How many of your target demographic live within that geographical boundary? What challenges and opportunities exist within that market?

2. Industry Overview
Begin with a macro-level examination of the industry. Include market size, growth trends, major players, and key factors influencing the industry's trajectory. Next, relate this data to how your entity fits into the market.

3. Target Market
Identify and describe your target market. Consider demographics, psychographics, and customer behavior to create a comprehensive profile of your ideal customer.
By developing detailed customer demographics, you can create a vivid

representation of your ideal customers. This information can be used to guide product development, marketing strategies, and overall business decisions.

Understanding your target market allows you to tailor your offerings to meet specific needs, effectively communicate value propositions, and establish a genuine connection with customers. This insight not only aids in customer acquisition but also fosters customer retention and loyalty, as businesses can continuously adapt to evolving market demands and preferences.

Ultimately, the ability to intimately understand and cater to the needs of the target market is a key driver of long-term business success.

4. Customer Needs and Pain Points

Next describe the needs, preferences, and pain points of your target customers. Highlight how your products or services address these specific customer challenges. By empathizing with your customers, you can identify the specific needs your products or services should address and the pain points they aim to alleviate.

This understanding goes beyond surface-level observations, delving into the emotional and practical aspects of customer experiences. Whether it's streamlining processes, enhancing convenience, or providing innovative solutions, businesses that adeptly identify and respond to customer needs and pain points are better equipped to forge meaningful connections with their audience.

This empathetic approach not only fosters customer satisfaction but also positions the business as a trusted partner in addressing the real-life challenges faced by its customers. As businesses align their offerings with these insights, they not only meet customer expectations but also lay the foundation for long-term loyalty and success.

5. Competitor Analysis

Conducting a competitor analysis is a pivotal step in developing a comprehensive business plan. This process involves a systematic examination of key competitors operating in the same industry or market segment.

A thorough competitor analysis goes beyond merely identifying rivals. It delves into their strengths, weaknesses, strategies, and market positioning. By assessing competitors' products, pricing strategies, distribution channels, and marketing tactics, you can better describe how your business fits into the market.

Understanding how competitors address customer needs and market trends helps you to identify opportunities for differentiation and strategic positioning for your own venture. A well-executed competitor analysis enables you to anticipate industry trends, assess potential threats, and ultimately craft informed strategies that enhance your competitive advantage.

It should be a dynamic process that empowers your business to adapt and respond proactively to the ever-evolving business environment, positioning you for success in a competitive marketplace.

6. Regulatory Environment

A comprehensive understanding of the regulatory environment is a fundamental aspect when crafting a business plan. This entails a thorough examination of the laws, regulations, and industry standards that govern the operation of a business within your specific jurisdiction.

The regulatory landscape can significantly impact various facets of a business, including licensing requirements, environmental compliance, labor laws, and consumer protection regulations.

Acknowledging and addressing these regulatory considerations is crucial for mitigating legal risks, ensuring ethical business practices, and maintaining compliance. A well-informed understanding of the regulatory environment not only demonstrates diligence to potential investors but also helps businesses navigate potential pitfalls and uncertainties. Moreover, it enables businesses to proactively incorporate compliance strategies into their operational plans, fostering a foundation of ethical and responsible business practices.

Consider how compliance may impact your business operations. You will probably require the assistance of an attorney familiar with regulations specific to your industry. A little bit of planning and foresight up-front can save you a lot of legal headaches later.

7. Market Trends

Analyzing market trends involves taking a systematic examination of current and emerging patterns in the industry, consumer behavior, and technology. To effectively analyze market trends, your business should stay abreast of changes in consumer preferences, technological advancements, and macroeconomic shifts.

This can be achieved through ongoing market research, monitoring industry reports, and leveraging data analytics. Understanding these trends allows businesses to anticipate shifts in demand, identify new opportunities, and align their products or services with evolving customer expectations.

By incorporating a thorough analysis of market trends into the business plan, you can demonstrate adaptability and a proactive approach to staying ahead in a dynamic business environment. Stay attuned to technological advancements, consumer preferences, and other factors shaping the industry.

8. SWOT Analysis

SWOT stands for Strengths, Weaknesses, Opportunities, and Threats.

A SWOT analysis offers a comprehensive assessment of your business's internal strengths and weaknesses, as well as external opportunities and threats. To initiate this analysis, you should first identify your entity's strengths, encompassing aspects like unique capabilities, resources, or competitive advantages.

Next, determine your weaknesses. These are areas where improvement or mitigation is needed. External factors are then assessed by identifying opportunities, such as emerging market trends, and threats, such as competitive pressures or regulatory changes.

The SWOT process involves candid self-reflection, consultation with key stakeholders, and a detailed examination of the business environment and your organization's place in the overall market.

The resulting analysis will help you to align your business and marketing strategies with both your internal capacities and external circumstances, resulting in informed decision-making and a more resilient business strategy.

Regular updates to the SWOT analysis ensure its relevance in guiding the business through dynamic market conditions.

Conducting Effective Market Research

As you can see, doing an effective Market Analysis will require a great deal of timely and accurate research. If you have no experience with doing market research or can't afford to have a market analysis firm do it for you, here are some basic items that will help you to understand the process better.

Primary Research

Primary research in market analysis involves the direct collection of data firsthand from original sources. This approach allows businesses to gather information tailored to their specific needs, offering insights into customer preferences, behaviors, and market dynamics.

Common methods of primary research include surveys, interviews, focus groups, and direct observations.

Surveys, conducted through questionnaires or online forms, allow businesses to gather quantitative data on a larger scale, while interviews and focus groups provide qualitative insights through in-depth conversations.

Direct observations involve firsthand scrutiny of consumer behavior or market conditions.

The advantage of primary research lies in its relevance and specificity to your company's unique context, offering a more accurate and targeted understanding of the market. However, it requires careful planning, execution, and analysis to ensure validity and reliability in the obtained data.

Internet technology has made the process somewhat easier, as surveys can be conducted online with a wide range of subjects without having to rely on mail-in surveys or face-to-face contact with potential customers.

Incorporating findings from primary research into a market analysis enhances the depth and authenticity of the insights, providing a solid foundation for informed business decisions.

Secondary Research

Secondary research utilizes existing data from reputable sources such as industry reports, market studies, and academic research. Incorporating secondary research into a market analysis involves leveraging existing data and information collected by others, such as industry reports, academic studies, and market analyses conducted by reputable sources.

Secondary research is a valuable complement to primary research, providing a broader context and a foundation of existing knowledge about the market. By reviewing literature, reports, and studies relevant to the industry, your business can gain insights into market trends, competitive landscapes, and consumer behavior without the need for direct data collection.

Secondary research is cost-effective and time-efficient, offering a quick snapshot of the market environment. The challenge lies in ensuring the reliability and relevance of the selected secondary sources. A meticulous review and critical analysis of the credibility and methodology of these sources are essential to draw accurate and meaningful conclusions. When combined with primary research, secondary research enriches the depth and breadth of an effective market analysis, providing a more comprehensive understanding of the business landscape.

Online Surveys and Analytics

Online surveys allow businesses to reach a wide audience quickly, collecting insights on consumer preferences, behaviors, and attitudes. These surveys can be customized to target specific demographics or customer segments, providing tailored information crucial for decision-making.

Additionally, leveraging web analytics tools enables businesses to scrutinize online consumer behavior, track website interactions, and measure digital marketing effectiveness. The data obtained through online surveys and analytics offer real-time and granular insights, empowering businesses to adapt strategies promptly based on evolving market dynamics.

This method not only facilitates a cost-effective means of data collection but also provides a technological edge in today's digital landscape. Integrating findings from online surveys and analytics into a market analysis enhances the precision and relevance of the overall strategic planning process.

4. Interviews and Expert Opinions

Interviews and expert opinions play a pivotal role in enriching the qualitative aspects of market analysis. Conducting interviews with industry experts, thought leaders, and key stakeholders provides a valuable qualitative dimension to the analysis.

These interactions can offer nuanced insights into industry trends, challenges, and potential opportunities that may not be apparent through quantitative data alone. Experts bring a wealth of experience and perspective, offering a qualitative depth that complements statistical findings.

Their opinions can help validate assumptions, identify emerging patterns, and uncover hidden market dynamics. Expert opinions add a layer of credibility to the market analysis, providing a more holistic understanding of the business environment.

By combining the wisdom of industry experts with other research methods, businesses can create a well-rounded and informed market analysis that guides strategic decision-making.

Key Components of the Market Analysis

The market analysis section of a business plan comprises several key components, each contributing to a comprehensive understanding of the business environment. These components include the Total Addressable Market (TAM), which estimates the overall demand for the product or service, providing a context for potential market share.

Target market size identifies the specific market segment the business aims to capture, considering geographic, demographic, and psychographic factors. Market segmentation involves dividing the market into segments based on relevant criteria, tailoring marketing strategies to each unique segment.

Analyzing the competitive landscape helps identify strengths, weaknesses, opportunities, and threats (SWOT) of key competitors. Customer personas create detailed representations of the ideal customers, incorporating demographics, interests, behaviors, and pain points.

Market share estimation, barriers to entry, and trends and growth projections complete the key components, forming a comprehensive analysis that guides strategic decision-making and business planning. Let's address each of these in a little more detail.

Total Addressable Market (TAM)

To determine TAM, you must first define the scope of your market, identifying the target audience and geographical boundaries. Subsequently, estimate the total potential market demand by multiplying the number of potential customers by the average revenue per customer. This involves a meticulous examination of available data, such as population statistics, industry reports, and relevant research studies.

It is essential to consider factors that may influence market size, such as market trends, economic conditions, and potential shifts in consumer behavior.

While TAM provides an overarching view of market potential, businesses should remain realistic in their estimations and be prepared to refine these figures as they gather more specific data during subsequent stages of market analysis.

Accurate TAM calculations serve as a foundation for strategic decision-making, helping businesses gauge market opportunities and appropriately position themselves within the industry.

To calculate your TAM:

1. *Target Market Size:* Determine the size of your specific target market. Consider geographical, demographic, and psychographic factors.
2. *Market Segmentation:* Divide the market into segments based on relevant criteria. Tailor your marketing strategies to the unique needs of each segment.
3. *Market Share:* Estimate your current or potential market share. Consider how you will capture and expand your share over time.
4. *Customer Persona:* Create detailed customer personas representing your ideal customers. Include demographics, interests, behaviors, and pain points.
5. *Competitive Landscape:* Provide a thorough analysis of key competitors. Identify areas where your business can differentiate and gain a competitive advantage.
6. *Barriers to Entry:* Identify potential barriers that could deter new entrants. Assess the ease or difficulty of entering the market.
7. *Market Trends and Growth Projections:* Highlight current and anticipated trends in the market. Provide growth projections based on industry dynamics.

Interpreting and Applying Market Analysis Findings

Once you have conducted a thorough examination of market trends, customer needs, competitive landscapes, and other key components, the next crucial step is to derive actionable insights.

Strategic insights are extracted by discerning patterns, correlations, and potential cause-and-effect relationships within the data. These insights guide decision-making processes, informing how your business positions itself, tailors its offerings, and allocates resources.

Risk assessment is another critical aspect, where you will identify potential challenges and develop mitigation strategies. Opportunities recognized during market analysis should be translated into innovative approaches, new product developments, or targeted marketing campaigns. With proper planning and finesse, you can turn risks into opportunities.

The pricing strategy, marketing messaging, and positioning are adjusted based on the findings, ensuring alignment with customer expectations and market realities. The true value of market analysis lies in its application. Done properly, it will transform information into strategies that drive your business towards success.

Some results of interpreting and applying a market analysis properly include:

1. **Strategic Insights**

    By interpreting and applying market analysis findings properly, businesses can identify and capitalize on emerging opportunities within the market. Whether it's a gap in the market, a growing trend, or an unmet customer need, recognizing and leveraging these opportunities allows businesses to position themselves as innovators and industry leaders.

    Understanding market dynamics enables your business to mitigate risks effectively. By identifying potential threats, such as changing consumer preferences or regulatory shifts, you can proactively develop strategies to navigate challenges and maintain resilience.

    Interpreting market analysis findings provides clarity on the competitive landscape. This insight allows businesses to differentiate themselves from competitors, refine their value proposition, and establish a unique selling proposition that resonates with their target audience.

    Additionally, businesses can fine-tune their marketing strategies, pricing models, and distribution channels based on a nuanced understanding of customer behaviors and preferences. Strategic insights from market analysis empower businesses to make informed decisions, allocate resources effectively, and understand how market dynamics influence your business strategy.

2. Risk Assessment

The insights gained from effective market analysis enable your entity to develop risk mitigation strategies, allowing you to proactively address challenges and enhance your resilience in the face of uncertainties.

Effectively assessing risks through market analysis is integral to strategic planning, guiding you in making informed decisions that safeguard your operations and long-term success. By scrutinizing market trends, competitive dynamics, and external factors, your business can identify potential risks that may impact your operations.

For example, changes in consumer preferences, technological advancements, or economic fluctuations can pose risks to market stability. Through competitor analysis, you can also assess the competitive landscape and potential challenges you may face from existing or emerging competitors. Regulatory factors, such as changes in industry standards or government policies, can also present risks.

By understanding customer needs and behaviors, your venture can anticipate shifts in demand and potential risks associated with product or service offerings.

3. Opportunity Recognition

Opportunities often manifest in unmet customer needs, gaps in the market, or emerging trends that align with a company's strengths. Through market segmentation, your business can pinpoint specific target audiences and tailor your products or services to meet the unique needs of these segments.

Competitor analysis allows you to identify areas where you can outperform or differentiate your venture from similar businesses in your target market, presenting opportunities for strategic positioning.

Through understanding the regulatory environment, you can also recognize opportunities that align with evolving industry standards. The insights gained from a market analysis provide a roadmap for your entity to capitalize on favorable market conditions, launch new products, or explore untapped market segments.

Ultimately, using a market analysis for opportunity recognition empowers your company to align your strategies with market dynamics, fostering innovation and sustainable growth.

4. Pricing Strategy

Understanding customer needs and behaviors through market analysis allows your venture to align pricing with the value customers attribute to your products or services. When interpreted correctly, a market analysis allows you to tailor pricing strategies to specific target audiences, optimizing pricing for different market segments.

Understanding the regulatory environment is also crucial to ensure compliance and avoid costly pricing-related legal challenges and litigation. Identification of cost structures through market analysis aids in establishing a pricing model that not only covers costs but also provides a competitive edge to your business.

Strategic pricing decisions, informed by market analysis, allow your business to position itself appropriately in the market, maximizing revenue while maintaining customer satisfaction and competitiveness.

5. Marketing and Positioning

When businesses tailor their marketing messages to address identified customer needs, they create a powerful connection with their target audience. Market analysis, especially customer segmentation and understanding their needs and pain points, provides valuable insights into what resonates with customers.

By aligning marketing messages with these insights, businesses can communicate directly to the desires and challenges of their audience, showcasing how their products or services uniquely fulfill those needs. This personalized approach not only enhances customer engagement but also establishes a brand as responsive and attuned to the market.

In response to competitor analysis, effective brand positioning becomes imperative. An effective market analysis helps you know the strengths and weaknesses of competitors so can strategically position your brand to highlight unique selling propositions and differentiate your venture in the market.

This might involve emphasizing product quality, superior customer service, competitive pricing, or innovative features. Knowing your own company's particular strengths and weaknesses can assist in this endeavor.

Positioning your brand effectively requires a nuanced understanding of what sets your business apart, and competitor analysis provides the necessary benchmarks for making informed decisions about how to communicate these differentiators to your target audience.

The synergy between tailoring marketing messages to customer needs and positioning your brand strategically based on competitor analysis creates a potent strategy for building a distinctive and competitive market presence. Businesses that master this balance not only resonate with their target audience but also carve out a unique space in the market, fostering brand loyalty and long-term success.

A robust Market Analysis is not merely a prerequisite for a business plan. It is the core upon which strategic business decisions hinge. It offers a panoramic view of the market, guiding your business to navigate complexities, seize opportunities, and fortify against challenges.

6 Marketing and Sales Strategy

A well-defined marketing and sales strategy is crucial for the success and growth of any business. The integration of a robust marketing and sales plan within a comprehensive business strategy is essential for attracting and retaining customers, driving revenue, and establishing a strong brand presence. In this chapter we'll discuss the key components and considerations for implementing an effective marketing and sales strategy in a business plan.

Before devising a marketing and sales strategy, it is imperative to have a comprehensive understanding of the market. Conducting thorough market research helps identify target customers, assess competitors, and understand industry trends. This knowledge forms the foundation for developing a strategy that aligns with the needs and preferences of the target audience.

Once the market is understood, a good business plan will need to define its target audience and segment it based on demographics, psychographics, and customer or client behavior. This segmentation allows for more personalized and targeted marketing efforts, increasing the likelihood of reaching and resonating with potential customers.

A compelling value proposition is the cornerstone of a successful marketing and sales strategy. It defines the unique value a product or service offers to customers. Clearly communicating this value proposition helps differentiate the business from competitors and provides a compelling reason for customers to choose the products or services your company offers and why customers would be attracted to your business over all the other ones in your market segment.

A diverse and integrated approach to marketing ensures that businesses reach their target audience through various channels. This may include digital marketing, social media, traditional advertising, content marketing, and public relations.

A multichannel strategy maximizes visibility and engagement, allowing businesses to connect with customers in different ways. The more diverse your marketing strategy, the more market penetration and the more likely target customers will see your advertising.

Digital marketing plays a pivotal role in any modern advertising strategy. Utilizing tools such as search engine optimization (SEO), social media marketing, email marketing, and online advertising can significantly enhance a business's online presence. These tools enable businesses to reach a broader audience, track performance metrics, and adjust strategies in real-time.

A well-structured sales funnel guides potential customers through the purchasing process, from awareness of your products and services to conversion (in other words, until they make a purchase). This involves creating awareness, generating interest, nurturing leads, and ultimately converting them into customers. Understanding the customer journey allows businesses to tailor their sales strategies at each stage of the funnel.

Customer Relationship Management (CRM) Systems

A CRM system is instrumental in managing customer interactions, tracking leads, and streamlining the sales process. By centralizing customer data, businesses can personalize their interactions, anticipate customer needs, and enhance overall customer satisfaction. A CRM system facilitates efficient communication and collaboration among sales and marketing teams.

To ensure the effectiveness of the marketing and sales strategy, businesses must regularly monitor and analyze key performance indicators. Metrics such as *conversion rates, customer acquisition cost, customer lifetime value,* and *return on investment* provide valuable insights into the success of the strategy. Continuous evaluation allows for adjustments and improvements based on performance data.

Conversion Rates

Conversion rates in a business plan refer to the percentage of potential customers or leads who take a desired action, such as making a purchase, signing up for a newsletter, or filling out a form. It is a key performance indicator (KPI) that measures the effectiveness of a business's marketing and sales efforts in turning prospects into customers.

There are various types of conversion rates, depending on the specific goal of the business. Here are a few common types:

Lead Conversion Rate: This measures the percentage of leads (potential customers) that convert into actual customers. For example, if a business generates 100 leads in a month and 10 of them make a purchase, the lead conversion rate would be 10%.

Visitor-to-Lead Conversion Rate: This ratio represents the percentage of website visitors who become leads by taking a specific action, such as filling out a contact form or downloading a whitepaper. If a website has 1,000 visitors and 50 of them submit a form, the visitor-to-lead conversion rate would be 5%.

Click-Through Rate (CTR) to Conversion Rate: In digital marketing, CTR measures the percentage of people who click on a specific link compared to the total number of people who saw it. The conversion rate in this context would measure the percentage of those who clicked through and then completed a desired action, such as making a purchase.

Cart Abandonment to Purchase Conversion Rate: For e-commerce businesses, this rate measures the percentage of users who add items to their shopping cart but do not complete the purchase. The goal is to convert abandoned carts into completed purchases. There are many plugins and apps that help online businesses to generate abandoned carts into sales. Your website developers should be able to help in this regard.

Monitoring and optimizing conversion rates are crucial for businesses because they provide insights into the efficiency of the sales and marketing funnel. Low conversion rates may indicate issues in the sales process, website design, or messaging, while high conversion rates suggest that the business is effectively engaging and persuading its audience.
In a business plan, understanding and setting goals for conversion rates help in assessing the feasibility and success of the marketing and sales strategies outlined in the plan. Additionally, ongoing analysis and adjustments based on conversion rate data contribute to the continuous improvement of business processes and outcomes.

Customer Acquisition Cost
Customer Acquisition Cost (CAC) is a pivotal metric that sheds light on the financial investment required to convert potential leads into loyal customers. Understanding this essential metric is a key part of any marketing and sales plan, and should therefore be incorporated into a comprehensive business plan.
Customer Acquisition Cost represents the total investment a business

makes to acquire a new customer. It encompasses various expenses related to marketing, sales, and other efforts aimed at attracting and converting leads. Calculating CAC is essential for businesses seeking to optimize their marketing strategies, allocate resources efficiently, and achieve a positive return on investment (ROI).

To grasp the concept of CAC fully, it is crucial to understand the components that contribute to this metric:

Marketing Expenses: This includes costs associated with advertising, promotions, content creation, and any other activities geared toward creating brand awareness and attracting potential customers.

Sales Expenses: This metric includes salaries, commissions, training, and tools used by the sales team. These expenses are critical for converting leads into paying customers.

Technology and Tools: This metric includes the costs of employing customer relationship management (CRM) systems, marketing automation tools, and other technologies that support customer acquisition efforts.

Incentives and Discounts: This includes expenditures tied to offering incentives, discounts, or promotions to entice potential customers to make a purchase.

The formula for calculating CAC is straightforward and provides a clear picture of the average cost incurred in acquiring each new customer:

Customer Acquisition Cost =
Cost of Sales and Marketing (including all items listed above)
divided by
Number of New Customers Acquired

This formula helps businesses evaluate the efficiency of their customer acquisition strategies and sets the foundation for strategic decision-making.

Resource Allocation: Understanding CAC enables businesses to allocate their marketing and sales budgets more effectively. By knowing the cost associated with acquiring a customer, companies can make data-driven decisions on where to invest their resources.

ROI Assessment: Evaluating CAC in relation to the lifetime value of a customer provides insights into the return on investment. This analysis is crucial for assessing the financial viability of customer acquisition strategies and ensuring that the cost of acquiring customers aligns with the value they bring over time.

Strategy Refinement: Continuous monitoring of CAC allows businesses to optimize their marketing and sales strategies. By identifying which channels or campaigns yield the best results, companies can refine their approach to maximize efficiency and minimize costs.

When crafting a business plan, it is imperative to dedicate a section to CAC. This section should outline the methodology used to calculate CAC, present historical data reflecting past performance, and provide projections for future customer acquisition costs. Additionally, the business plan should detail how the company plans to optimize CAC over time through strategic adjustments.

Knowing Customer Acquisition Cost empowers businesses to make informed decisions regarding budget allocation, resource management, and overall marketing strategy. By incorporating a comprehensive analysis of CAC into the business plan, companies position themselves for success by fostering sustainable growth and building lasting relationships with their customers. Understanding and mastering the nuances of CAC is a key driver of long-term business success.

Customer Lifetime Value (CLV) quantifies

Customer Lifetime Value (CLV) quantifies the total predicted revenue a customer is expected to generate over the entire duration of their relationship with a company. It goes beyond the immediate transactional value of a customer and factors in their potential for repeated purchases, brand loyalty, and the overall financial contribution they make to the business over time.

Understanding Customer Lifetime Value (CLV) aids a business in strategic marketing decisions and should therefore be included in any business plan. Here are some strategical reasons why understanding CLV is important:

Resource Allocation: Understanding the CLV helps businesses allocate resources effectively. Companies can tailor their marketing and customer retention strategies based on the value different customer segments bring over their lifetime.

Acquisition Costs: When juxtaposed with Customer Acquisition Cost (CAC), CLV helps businesses evaluate the return on investment. If the cost of acquiring a customer is lower than their lifetime value, it indicates a potentially lucrative business strategy.

Tailored Marketing: CLV aids in segmenting customers based on their potential lifetime value. This allows businesses to create targeted marketing campaigns for high-value customers, enhancing the likelihood of customer retention and upselling.

Customer Prioritization: By identifying and prioritizing high CLV customers, businesses can focus on building stronger relationships with those who contribute significantly to long-term revenue.

Financial Health: CLV is a crucial indicator of a company's financial health. Monitoring CLV over time enables businesses to assess the effectiveness of their customer retention strategies and overall business performance.

Revenue Predictions: CLV provides a basis for predicting future revenue streams, aiding in long-term financial planning and forecasting.

Service Personalization: Businesses can use CLV insights to tailor their services to meet the specific needs and expectations of high-value customers, thereby enhancing customer satisfaction and loyalty.

Retention Strategies: Understanding CLV guides the development of effective customer retention strategies. By focusing on building long-term relationships, businesses can reduce churn and maximize customer value.

Investment Attractiveness: In a business plan, highlighting a solid understanding of CLV makes a company more attractive to investors. It demonstrates a strategic approach to customer management and financial sustainability.

Stakeholder Assurance: Stakeholders, including employees and partners, gain confidence in a business's longevity and growth potential when the business plan showcases a robust CLV strategy.

Market Differentiation: Businesses that prioritize CLV often gain a competitive advantage. By demonstrating a commitment to long-term customer relationships, companies can distinguish themselves in the market and foster customer loyalty.

Incorporating a comprehensive analysis of Customer Lifetime Value into a business plan indicates a forward-thinking approach and a strategic vision. It assures stakeholders that the company is not solely focused on short-term gains but is committed to building lasting and profitable relationships with its customer base. Understanding and leveraging CLV is a key element in achieving sustained success.

Return on Investment (ROI)
Return on Investment is a financial metric that evaluates the profitability of an investment relative to its cost. It is expressed as a percentage and provides insights into the efficiency of capital allocation.

The formula for calculating ROI is:

$$ROI = (Net\ Profit \div Cost\ of\ Investment) \times 100$$

This metric is not only a measure of financial performance but also a key indicator of the success and viability of various business initiatives. Return on Investment calculations aid strategic decision-making and business planning in the following domains:

Resource Allocation: ROI guides businesses in allocating resources effectively. By assessing the potential returns on different investment options, organizations can prioritize projects or strategies that promise the highest returns.

Risk Management: Understanding ROI allows businesses to evaluate the potential risks associated with an investment. Projects with a high ROI may be more appealing, but a comprehensive analysis helps identify and mitigate potential risks.

Financial Health: ROI serves as a barometer for a company's financial health. Consistently low or negative ROI may indicate the need for strategic adjustments, while a positive ROI demonstrates the effectiveness of business initiatives.

Project Success: Evaluating the ROI of specific projects or campaigns helps measure their success. This insight is crucial for refining strategies and replicating successful approaches in the future.

Business Attractiveness: Investors scrutinize ROI when assessing the attractiveness of a business. A well-understood and effectively communicated ROI strategy in a business plan instills confidence in potential investors, showcasing a thoughtful and financially prudent approach.

Risk Mitigation: Investors are by nature risk-averse. They seek the greatest amount of potential revenue with the least amount of risk. A strong ROI track record can mitigate concerns, making a business more appealing for investors.

Marketing and Advertising: ROI is particularly crucial in marketing and advertising efforts. By tracking the ROI of different channels and campaigns, businesses can optimize their marketing spend, focusing on channels that deliver the best returns.

Technology and Infrastructure: Assessing the ROI of technology investments and infrastructure enhancements helps in prioritizing initiatives that contribute most significantly to overall business objectives.

Sustainability: Understanding ROI facilitates long-term planning by ensuring that investments align with the organization's strategic goals. Sustainable growth requires ongoing evaluation of ROI to adapt to changing market dynamics.

Adaptability: ROI insights enable businesses to adapt to evolving market trends. By continuously evaluating the performance of investments, organizations can reallocate resources to capitalize on emerging opportunities.

When incorporating ROI into the Business Plan, there should be a clearly defined methodology for doing so, including explanations for all the elements included in the business plan. Some of the components for consideration in this clear and concise explanation should be:

Calculation Explanation: A business plan should clearly outline the methodology used for ROI calculations. This transparency instills confidence in stakeholders and provides a clear understanding of how the organization evaluates the success of its investments. Conversely, if the ROI methodology is left unclear, it would be a major reason for a potential investor to lack trust and therefore lack incentives to invest in your venture.

Assumptions and Considerations: Include a section detailing the assumptions and considerations made in ROI calculations. This enhances the plan's credibility and provides context for stakeholders. Make sure that your assumptions and considerations are reasonable to any objective observer. Avoid the tendency to exaggerate in an effort to make your business look more attractive. Dishonesty in your assumptions can have the opposite of the effect intended.

Past Performance: Presenting historical ROI data showcases the business's track record and helps stakeholders understand how previous investments have contributed to overall success. If you are a new business, you can include data on how similar businesses have performed in the past. This can be especially effective for new businesses, as it is an opportunity to explain how your business will do things differently than the others in the field.

Future Projections: Including ROI projections demonstrates the organization's strategic vision and financial forecasting. It highlights the anticipated returns from future investments and the expected impact on overall profitability.

Investors and other stakeholders always seek to minimize risk and maximize ROI. For this reason, it is also crucial to include risk mitigation strategies in your business plan. Essential elements for risk mitigation include:

Contingency Plans: Acknowledge potential risks and uncertainties in the business plan and outline contingency plans. This demonstrates a proactive approach to risk management and instills confidence in stakeholders. Don't try to hide or conceal any potential risks. Strategic investors will probably already know what many of the potential risks are, and trying to conceal these risks will make potential investors shy away from your organization.

Sensitivity Analysis: Consider incorporating sensitivity analysis to assess how changes in assumptions or market conditions may impact ROI. This adds depth to the business plan by addressing potential scenarios, and it demonstrates that you are a forward-thinking strategist.

A Return on Investment section in your business plan not only reflects the financial health of the organization but also guides strategic decision-making. A comprehensive grasp of ROI empowers businesses to allocate resources wisely, evaluate performance, attract investors, optimize operations, and plan for long-term sustainability. By incorporating clear methodologies, historical data, and risk mitigation strategies into the business plan, organizations can showcase a robust understanding of ROI, building confidence and setting the stage for informed and successful business endeavors.

Implementing an effective marketing and sales strategy is fundamental for the success of any business. By understanding the market, defining target audiences, crafting compelling value propositions, and leveraging digital tools, businesses can create a robust plan that attracts and retains customers.

The integration of a sales funnel for online marketing, CRM systems, and ongoing monitoring of KPIs ensures adaptability and sustained success. A well-executed marketing and sales strategy not only drives revenue but also establishes a strong brand presence and fosters long-term customer relationships. It also enhances investor confidence in your entity and entices them to be more willing to invest in your venture, so spend a lot of time crafting this section of your business plan.

And of course, don't forget that a business plan itself is a type of marketing tool. In addition to being an overview of your business, a business plan can be used to market your venture to investors and other stakeholders, therefore the marketing and advertising section of your business plan is critical to success.

7 Organizational Structure

A business's organizational structure outlines the hierarchy, roles, and relationships within the company, providing a framework for efficient operations and effective decision-making. Every detailed business plan should contain a section on the proposed entity's business and organizational structure.

An organizational structure is akin to a blueprint that shapes the way a business functions. It establishes lines of authority, communication channels, and the division of responsibilities. A meticulously crafted structure is critical for several reasons:

Clarity of Roles and Responsibilities: A well-defined organizational structure ensures that each member of the team understands their role and responsibilities, minimizing confusion and promoting accountability by establishing a "chain of command" for the organization. This clarity fosters a sense of purpose and direction among employees.

Efficient Communication: Effective communication is the lifeblood of any organization. A well-designed structure streamlines communication channels, preventing information bottlenecks and ensuring that vital information reaches the right people in a timely manner.

Decision-Making Agility: The hierarchy established by the organizational structure facilitates efficient decision-making. Clear lines of authority empower employees at different levels to make informed decisions within their areas of responsibility, promoting agility and responsiveness.

Employee Morale and Productivity: When employees know where they fit into the larger picture, they feel a sense of belonging and purpose. This, in turn, boosts morale and productivity. A hierarchical structure with well-defined career paths motivates employees to strive for excellence and advancement.

Types of Organizational Structures

There are various organizational structures, each with its advantages and disadvantages. Common types include:

Functional Structure

A functional structure is a type of organizational structure in which the company is divided into distinct functional areas or departments based on specialized functions or tasks. Each department is responsible for specific functions, and employees within each department typically have similar skills and expertise. This structure is designed to enhance efficiency and expertise in each functional area. Here are the key characteristics and advantages of a functional structure:

Functional Departments: The organization is divided into functional areas such as marketing, finance, operations, human resources, and so on. Each department is responsible for specific tasks related to its function.

Clear Hierarchy: There is a clear hierarchy with a top-level executive overseeing the entire organization, and lower-level managers responsible for each functional area. This helps in maintaining a clear chain of command.

Specialization: Employees within each functional area are specialists in their respective fields. This specialization allows for in-depth knowledge and expertise in specific functions.

Efficiency: Functional structures are often efficient because they allow employees to focus on specific tasks and become experts in their areas. This can lead to streamlined processes and increased productivity.

Communication within Departments: Communication is generally more straightforward within departments, as employees share similar skills and knowledge. This can lead to effective collaboration and problem-solving within functional units.

There are certain advantages to using a functional structure. These advantages include, but are not limited to:

Expertise and Specialization: The functional structure allows employees to specialize in their respective areas, leading to a high level of expertise. This can result in higher-quality outputs.

Clear Reporting Lines: The hierarchy is well-defined, making it clear who reports to whom. This clarity can facilitate decision-making and communication.

Cost-Efficiency: By grouping similar functions together, companies can achieve economies of scale and reduce redundancies. This can lead to cost savings in the long run.

Training and Development: Employees within functional areas can receive specialized training and development opportunities tailored to their roles, fostering continuous improvement.

Applicability to Large Organizations: Functional structures are well-suited for large organizations with diverse functions. It allows for effective management of multiple tasks and functions.

There are certain disadvantages to using a functional structure as well. These disadvantages include, but are not limited to:

Communication Between Departments: While communication within departments is efficient, communication between departments can sometimes be a challenge. Silos may form, hindering cross-functional collaboration. This enhances the possibility of *groupthink*. Groupthink occurs when there is a practice of thinking or making decisions as a group in a way that discourages creativity or individual responsibility. It usually occurs when people are unwilling to go against the group or when one individual with a dominant personality takes charge and silences any dissenting voices.

Rigidity: Functional structures can be rigid and slow to adapt to changes. This might be a disadvantage in industries where flexibility and quick decision-making are crucial.

Coordination Issues: Coordinating activities across different functional areas may require additional effort. Ensuring alignment and collaboration between departments is essential. This means that the process of communication between departments will need to be especially well-established and clearly defined.

Limited Focus on Overall Organizational Goals: Employees may become overly focused on their specific functions and may lose sight of the organization's overall goals. This lack of holistic perspective can be a drawback.

A functional structure is a common organizational design that arranges activities based on specialized functions. While it has clear advantages in terms of expertise and efficiency, it also comes with challenges related to communication and adaptability. Be aware of these when writing this section of your business plan.

Divisional Structure

A divisional structure is a type of organizational structure in which a company is divided into semi-autonomous units or divisions, each operating as its own entity with its own set of functions. Each division is responsible for a specific product line, geographic region, customer segment, or business unit.

This structure allows for greater flexibility and responsiveness to the unique needs and challenges of different markets or products.

Here are the key characteristics and advantages of a divisional structure:

Divisional Units: The organization is divided into distinct divisions, each with its own set of functions and responsibilities. Divisions can be organized based on products, geography, customer segments, or other criteria.

Autonomy: Divisions operate with a degree of autonomy, allowing them to make decisions tailored to their specific markets or products. This autonomy promotes flexibility and responsiveness to local conditions.

Divisional Heads: Each division is typically headed by a manager or executive who has authority over the division's operations. These leaders are responsible for the division's performance and strategic decisions.

Resource Allocation: Resources such as human capital, finances, and technology are often allocated to divisions based on their specific needs and strategic priorities. This ensures that each division has the necessary resources to succeed.

Product or Market Focus: The divisional structure allows for a clear focus on specific products, markets, or customer segments. This specialization can lead to a deeper understanding of the unique requirements of each area.

There are certain advantages to using a divisional structure. These advantages include, but are not limited to:

Market Responsiveness: Divisions can respond quickly to changes in their respective markets or industries, adapting strategies and operations to meet local demands.

Clear Accountability: Each division operates as a semi-autonomous unit, which fosters clear lines of accountability. Divisional managers are directly responsible for the performance of their divisions.

Specialization: Divisional structures allow for specialization within each division, leading to a high level of expertise in specific products or markets.

Flexibility: The decentralized nature of the divisional structure provides flexibility in decision-making, making it easier to adapt to diverse market conditions.

Motivation and Engagement: Divisional managers and employees may feel a greater sense of ownership and motivation because they are responsible for the success of their specific division.

There are certain disadvantages to using a divisional structure as well. These disadvantages include, but are not limited to:

Coordination Issues: Coordinating activities and ensuring alignment across different divisions can be challenging. There may be a need for effective communication and collaboration mechanisms.

Duplication of Efforts: There is a risk of duplication of efforts and resources across divisions, especially if there is insufficient coordination and sharing of best practices. This is another area where clear communication channels are not only important, but imperative.

Cost Inefficiencies: While divisions can be efficient in their operations, there may be higher overall costs due to the duplication of certain functions, such as administrative or support services.

Strategic Inconsistency: Ensuring consistency in the overall strategic direction of the organization can be challenging when divisions have a higher degree of autonomy.

A divisional structure is a decentralized organizational design that organizes a company into semi-autonomous divisions. This structure is particularly effective for businesses with diverse product lines, multiple geographic locations, or varied customer segments. While it offers advantages in terms of flexibility and market responsiveness, it also presents challenges related to coordination and strategic consistency. Be sure to make these clear when you write the Organizational Structure section of your business plan.

Matrix Structure

A matrix structure is a type of organizational structure that combines elements of both *functional* and *divisional* structures. In a matrix structure, employees have dual reporting relationships, typically to both a functional manager and a project or product manager. This structure is designed to capitalize on the strengths of both functional and divisional structures, providing flexibility, efficient resource utilization, and the ability to respond quickly to changing priorities.

Here are the key characteristics and features of a matrix structure:

Dual Reporting: Employees in a matrix structure report to both a functional manager (based on their specialization or expertise) and a project or product manager (based on the specific project or product they are working on).

Functional and Project/Product Teams: The business is organized into functional teams (e.g., marketing, finance, engineering) and project or product teams, each with its own manager. Employees contribute to both types of teams simultaneously.

Flexible Resource Allocation: Resources, including employees, can be flexibly allocated to different projects or products based on the organization's needs. This allows for efficient utilization of specialized skills across various projects.

Cross-Functional Collaboration: The matrix structure encourages collaboration across functional lines. Employees with different expertise work together on projects, bringing diverse perspectives and skills to the table.

Adaptability: The matrix structure is well-suited for organizations that operate in dynamic environments with rapidly changing priorities. It allows for quick adaptation to new projects or shifting business requirements.

There are certain advantages to using a matrix structure. These advantages include, but are not limited to:

Resource Efficiency: The matrix structure enables organizations to efficiently utilize resources by sharing specialized skills across projects or products without the need for duplicating functional departments.

Enhanced Communication: Cross-functional collaboration promotes better communication and understanding between different parts of the organization. This can lead to improved problem-solving and decision-making.

Flexibility: The dual-reporting system allows for flexibility in managing both functional responsibilities and project-related tasks. This adaptability is valuable in industries with constantly changing requirements.

Employee Development: Employees in a matrix structure often have the opportunity to work on diverse projects, contributing to their professional development and exposure to different aspects of the business.

Project Focus: The structure is well-suited for organizations that operate on a project or product basis, allowing for a dedicated focus on specific initiatives.

There are certain disadvantages to using a matrix structure as well. These disadvantages include, but are not limited to:

Role Ambiguity: Employees may experience role ambiguity or confusion due to dual reporting relationships. It is important to establish clear expectations and communication channels.

Conflict of Priorities: Conflicts may arise between functional and project managers over resource allocation and priorities. Effective communication and coordination are crucial to address these challenges.

Complex Decision-Making: Decision-making can be more complex in a matrix structure, especially when multiple managers are involved. It requires a collaborative and transparent decision-making process.

Management Overhead: Managing a matrix structure can be resource-intensive, requiring effective coordination, communication, and conflict resolution. This can result in increased management overhead.

Potential for Power Struggles: The dual reporting relationships may lead to power struggles between functional and project managers. Establishing clear lines of authority and conflict resolution mechanisms is essential in a matrix structure.

A matrix structure is a hybrid organizational design that combines elements of both functional and divisional structures. It is suitable for organizations facing dynamic environments and complex projects, offering advantages in resource efficiency, flexibility, and cross-functional collaboration.

However, it also presents challenges related to role ambiguity, conflict resolution, and management complexity. The success of a matrix structure depends on effective communication, clear expectations, and robust coordination mechanisms.

Flat Structure

A flat structure, also known as a horizontal or decentralized structure, is an organizational design that minimizes levels of hierarchy and emphasizes a broader span of control.

In a flat structure, there are fewer layers of management between the top leadership and the front-line employees. This approach is often characterized by open communication, a streamlined decision-making process, and increased autonomy for employees.

Here are the key characteristics and features of a flat structure:

Fewer Hierarchical Levels: A flat structure has a limited number of hierarchical levels. It typically consists of a small top management team overseeing a larger number of employees, resulting in a shorter chain of command.

Wide Span of Control: Managers in a flat structure have a wide span of control, meaning they oversee a larger number of employees. This allows for more direct communication and interaction between managers and their teams.

Open Communication: Communication flows more directly between top management and employees, fostering a culture of open communication. There are fewer intermediaries, promoting a sense of transparency and accessibility.

Empowerment and Autonomy: Employees in a flat structure often have more autonomy and decision-making authority. This empowerment can lead to increased job satisfaction and a greater sense of responsibility.

Quick Decision-Making: With fewer layers of management, decision-making tends to be quicker and more agile. There is less bureaucracy, enabling organizations to respond rapidly to changing circumstances.

Collaboration: Collaboration is encouraged across different levels of the organization. The emphasis on open communication and reduced hierarchy promotes a collaborative and team-oriented culture.

There are certain advantages to using a flat structure. These advantages include, but are not limited to:

Quick Decision-Making: Flat structures are known for their agility in decision-making. Without numerous layers of approval, decisions can be made more rapidly, allowing the organization to respond swiftly to market changes.

Improved Communication: The reduced hierarchy fosters direct communication between top management and employees, creating a more transparent and open work environment.

Employee Empowerment: Employees in a flat structure often have more autonomy and responsibility, which can lead to higher job satisfaction and increased motivation.

Cost-Efficiency: With fewer management layers, there is a potential for cost savings. Organizations can operate more efficiently by eliminating unnecessary bureaucratic positions.

Flexibility: Flat structures are adaptable to change, making them well-suited for dynamic and fast-paced environments. The streamlined decision-making process allows for quick adjustments to market conditions.

There are certain disadvantages to using a flat structure as well. These disadvantages include, but are not limited to:

Limited Career Advancement: The flatter hierarchy may limit traditional career advancement opportunities. Employees may have fewer promotional levels to progress through.

Overburdened Managers: Managers in flat structures may experience a heavier workload due to a wider span of control. This could potentially lead to burnout if not managed effectively.

Role Ambiguity: With fewer layers of management, there might be a lack of clarity regarding roles and responsibilities, potentially leading to role ambiguity among employees.

Dependency on Managerial Skills: The success of a flat structure is often dependent on the managerial skills of those in leadership positions. Effective communication, decision-making, and leadership become even more crucial.

Resistance to Change: Employees accustomed to traditional hierarchical structures may resist the shift to a flat structure. A cultural shift and effective change management are necessary for a smooth transition.

A flat structure is characterized by a streamlined hierarchy with few levels of management. While it offers advantages such as quick decision-making and improved communication, it also presents challenges related to career advancement, managerial workload, and potential resistance to change.
The suitability of a flat structure depends on the organization's size, culture, and the nature of its operations.

Implementation Challenges and Solutions

Despite the benefits, implementing and maintaining an effective organizational structure can pose challenges. Resistance to change, unclear communication, and the need for periodic adjustments are common issues. To address these challenges, businesses should invest in:

Change Management Strategies: Implementing a new organizational structure often requires a cultural shift. Change management strategies, such as clear communication, employee training, and leadership support, can help ease the transition.

Regular Evaluation and Adjustment: A business's environment is dynamic, and so too should be its organizational structure. Regular evaluations, feedback loops, and a willingness to adjust the structure as needed are crucial for long-term success.

Composing the Organizational Structure

When writing the Organizational Structure section of your business plan there are several steps and considerations involved. If you follow these steps you will be well on your way to creating a comprehensive and strategic organizational structure section for a business plan.

These steps include:

1. Understand the Business Model and Goals

Before delving into the specifics of organizational structure, it is imperative to have a deep understanding of the business model and goals. This understanding includes knowing what type of entity the business is (see the *Types of Business Entity* section that follows). Consider the industry, market positioning, and long-term objectives. This foundational knowledge will inform decisions about the most suitable organizational structure to support the company's vision.

2. Define Leadership and Key Positions

Clearly articulate the leadership team and key positions within the organization. Identify the CEO, department heads, and any other critical roles. Provide concise profiles that highlight the qualifications and experience of key personnel. You may wish to create an organizational flowchart for this section. This information gives potential investors and stakeholders confidence in the leadership's ability to drive the business forward.

3. Choose an Appropriate Organizational Structure

Selecting the right organizational structure is a pivotal decision. Depending on the nature and scale of the business, opt for a *functional, divisional, matrix,* or *flat* structure as outlined in the previous section. The size of your business will dictate the type of organizational structure needed. A small business should be fine with a flat structure, while a complex organization might need one of the other types. Justify the choice by explaining how it aligns with the company's goals, enhances efficiency, and promotes effective communication and decision-making.

4. Hierarchy and Reporting Lines
Clearly outline the hierarchy and reporting lines within the organization. Define who reports to whom, illustrating the flow of authority and communication. A visual representation, such as an organizational chart, can be an effective tool to convey this information in a clear and accessible manner.

5. Roles and Responsibilities
Detail the roles and responsibilities associated with each position in the organizational structure. Provide a comprehensive overview of the duties, expectations, and key performance indicators for each role. This section ensures that every team member understands their contribution to the overall success of the company. You may wish to include job descriptions as an appendix in your business plan, or at least have them available should investors or other stakeholders be interested.

6. Communication Channels
Describe the communication channels within the organization. Highlight regular communication mechanisms, such as team meetings, project updates, and performance reviews. Effective communication is vital for a cohesive and productive workforce, and addressing this in the business plan demonstrates a commitment to transparent and open communication practices. The Connected Culture Report published in 2020 states that 86% of employees and executives cite the lack of effective collaboration and communication as the main causes of workplace failures. You can go a long way towards building confidence in your venture by developing an effective communication strategy with well-defined communication channels.

7. Adaptability and Growth Plans
Anticipate future growth and changes in the business environment. Discuss how the organizational structure can adapt to accommodate expansion, acquisitions, or shifts in market dynamics. Demonstrating foresight in this area reflects strategic thinking and long-term planning.

8. Risk Mitigation Strategies
Identify potential risks associated with the chosen organizational structure and propose mitigation strategies. Address challenges related to communication breakdowns, resistance to change, or disruptions in leadership. Investors and stakeholders appreciate a business plan that acknowledges potential pitfalls and outlines plans for risk mitigation.

The basic formula for troubleshooting risk is to first identify the problem, then anticipate possible solutions, then choose the best one and implement it. After implementing your proposed solution, analyze the results. Continue this process until you find an effective solution.

Types of Business Entity

Choosing the right business entity is a pivotal decision that significantly impacts a company's structure, liability, taxation, and overall operational dynamics. Limited Liability Companies (LLCs) and Corporations stand out as two distinct business entities, each with its own set of advantages and considerations. A good Organizational Structure section of an effective business plan should be able to focus on the characteristics, benefits, and differences between LLCs and Corporations, and why a particular legal structure was chosen for your business. Writing this section effectively empowers entrepreneurs to make informed decisions when investing.

Limited Liability Company (LLC)

A Limited Liability Company, or LLC, is a flexible and popular business structure that combines elements of a partnership and a corporation. Key features of an LLC include:

Limited Liability: The primary advantage of an LLC is the limited liability it affords to its members. This means that the personal assets of the members are generally protected from business debts and liabilities. With an LLC, if your business gets sued they can generally only come after your business property and not your personal private property.

Flexibility in Management: LLCs offer flexibility in management structures. Members can choose to manage the company themselves or appoint managers. This adaptability allows for a more customized approach to leadership.

Pass-Through Taxation: One of the significant benefits of an LLC is its pass-through taxation. Profits and losses are passed through to the members, who report this income on their individual tax returns. This avoids the double taxation associated with corporations.

Ease of Formation and Administration: Setting up an LLC is relatively straightforward compared to other business structures. There are fewer formalities, and ongoing administrative requirements are generally less burdensome.

Corporation

A Corporation is a distinct legal entity that exists separately from its owners (shareholders). There are two main types of corporations: C Corporations and S Corporations. Key features of corporations include:

Limited Liability: Similar to an LLC, shareholders in a corporation enjoy limited liability. Their personal assets are typically protected from the company's debts and legal liabilities.

Perpetual Existence: A significant advantage of a corporation is its perpetual existence. The business continues to exist even if shareholders change or pass away, providing stability and continuity.

Ease of Capital Acquisition: Corporations can easily raise capital by selling shares of stock. This makes them an attractive option for businesses with ambitious expansion plans or those seeking significant investment.

Separation of Ownership and Management: In a corporation, the owners (shareholders) can separate their roles from management. The board of directors oversees strategic decisions, while officers and managers handle day-to-day operations.

Double Taxation: Unlike an LLC, a C Corporation is subject to double taxation. Corporate profits are taxed at the corporate level, and then shareholders are taxed on any dividends they receive. However, S Corporations can avoid double taxation by electing pass-through taxation.

Choosing Between LLC and Corporation

The choice between an LLC and a Corporation depends on various factors, including the nature of the business, the number of owners, tax considerations, and long-term goals. LLCs are often favored by small to medium-sized businesses seeking flexibility and simplicity, while corporations are suitable for those aiming for significant growth and access to capital.

Understanding the nuances of LLCs and Corporations is paramount when writing your Organizational Structure section of an effective business plan. Both structures offer unique advantages, and the decision hinges on the specific needs and goals of the business. If you can discuss the type of entity chosen for your business and the reason it was chosen, you'll build investor confidence.

Writing the Organizational Structure

The Organizational Structure section of a business plan is a strategic roadmap that shapes the company's trajectory. By understanding the business model, defining key positions, choosing an appropriate structure, and addressing communication and growth considerations, businesses can present a compelling and well-thought-out organizational structure section. This not only instills confidence in potential investors but also sets the stage for operational excellence and sustained success.

An effective organizational structure is a guiding compass. Whether a business adopts a functional, divisional, matrix, or flat structure, the key is to align the organization with its goals and values. As your business continues to evolve, so too should your organizational structures, adapting to new challenges and opportunities.

8 Operations Plan

An operations plan is a detailed document that delineates how a company will conduct its daily operations to achieve its strategic objectives. It serves as a blueprint for managing resources, processes, and activities to ensure efficiency and productivity. The primary purpose of an operations plan is to provide a clear understanding of how the business will function on a day-to-day basis and how it will deliver value to its customers.

There are several key components of a successful and effective business Operations Plan. These include:

Business Processes
Clearly define the core processes that drive your business. Outline the steps involved in product/service development, delivery, and customer service. This section should provide a comprehensive view of the operational workflow.

Core processes serve as the backbone or any organization, guiding daily operations, optimizing efficiency, and ensuring that the organization can deliver products or services consistently.

Clearly defined core processes enable businesses to operate with efficiency. By breaking down complex operations into well-defined steps, organizations can identify bottlenecks, streamline activities, and eliminate unnecessary tasks.

Well-defined processes contribute to consistent outputs, ensuring that products or services meet a predetermined standard of quality. This consistency is vital for building customer trust and loyalty.

Understanding core processes helps in allocating resources effectively. By identifying key areas of operation, businesses can optimize their workforce, technology, and other resources to maximize productivity.

Clearly defined processes make it easier for businesses to adapt to changes and scale their operations. When processes are well-documented, it becomes simpler to introduce new technologies, integrate additional services, or expand into new markets.

Begin by identifying the key functional areas within your organization. These could include product development, marketing, sales, customer service, and more. Clearly outline the purpose and goals of each functional area.

Create detailed process maps for each identified functional area. Break down each process into individual steps, illustrating the flow of activities from start to finish. Use visual aids such as flowcharts to enhance understanding.

Document standard operating procedures for each process. SOPs provide a comprehensive guide for employees, ensuring that everyone follows the same set of guidelines. Include key performance indicators (KPIs) to measure process effectiveness.

Clearly define roles and responsibilities within each process. Assign specific tasks to individuals or teams and establish communication channels to ensure seamless collaboration. This clarity helps avoid confusion and promotes accountability.

Implement a system for continuous monitoring of processes. Regularly assess performance metrics and gather feedback from employees involved in the processes. Use this information to identify areas for improvement and make necessary adjustments.

Provide comprehensive training for employees involved in core processes. Ensure that team members understand the importance of their roles and how their activities contribute to the overall success of the organization.

By following systematic steps such as process mapping, documentation, and continuous improvement, businesses can enhance their overall performance.

Facilities and Equipment

Specify the physical assets required for your operations. This includes facilities, machinery, technology, and other infrastructure necessary for the smooth functioning of your business.

Specifying the physical assets required for operations is a crucial step that directly impacts your organization's efficiency and productivity. Clearly outlining physical assets in a business plan provides insights into the process of specifying these assets to ensure operational excellence.

Begin by clearly defining physical assets assists in efficient resource allocation. This includes determining the type and quantity of equipment, machinery, technology, and facilities necessary for smooth business operations.

A precise list of physical assets contributes to operational efficiency as well. When they know what their physical assets are, businesses can strategically organize and optimize these assets, reducing bottlenecks, and ensuring that each plays a defined role in the overall operational process.

With a comprehensive list of physical assets, organizations can accurately estimate the costs associated with acquisition, maintenance, and depreciation of each. This information is vital for budgeting and financial planning, allowing for better control over expenditures.

Understanding the physical assets required for operations helps in identifying potential risks related to equipment failure, technological obsolescence, or facility issues such as maintenance and upkeep. This knowledge enables businesses to implement effective risk mitigation strategies that can have a tremendous impact on Return on Investment (ROI).

The steps to specify physical assets in a business plan include:

1. Conduct a Needs Assessment

Begin by conducting a comprehensive needs assessment. Evaluate the requirements of each operational area, considering factors such as production capacity, technological advancements, and future scalability.

2. List Essential Equipment and Machinery

Clearly list the essential equipment and machinery needed for your operations. Include details such as specifications, quantities, and expected usage. Ensure that the chosen equipment aligns with industry standards and technological advancements.

3. Technology Infrastructure

Identify the technological infrastructure required to support your operations. This may include hardware, software, communication systems, and network capabilities. Address how these technologies will integrate into your overall operational framework.

4. Facility Requirements

Specify the physical space needed for your operations. Outline facility requirements in terms of size, location, layout, and any specialized features. Consider factors such as safety regulations, accessibility, and environmental impact.

5. Maintenance and Upkeep Plans

Detail plans for the maintenance and upkeep of physical assets. This includes scheduled maintenance routines, replacement strategies, and protocols for handling unforeseen breakdowns. Clearly define responsibilities for asset management.

6. Compliance and Regulations

Consider any regulatory requirements related to your physical assets. Ensure that your chosen equipment and facilities comply with industry standards, safety regulations, and environmental guidelines. Address any permits or certifications needed.

By following systematic steps such as needs assessment, listing equipment, and detailing maintenance plans, your business plan will demonstrate a clear understanding of your core business processes that will be attractive to investors and other stakeholders.

Supply Chain Management

Detailing the procurement, inventory management, and distribution processes in a business plan is essential for creating a comprehensive and well-organized operational strategy. These processes are critical components that directly impact a company's ability to meet customer demand efficiently.

The key steps involved in detailing these processes within a business plan include:

1. Procurement Process

Begin by identifying potential suppliers and partners. Clearly outline the criteria for selection, such as reliability, cost-effectiveness, and adherence to quality standards. Consider establishing long-term relationships for consistency.

Next, clearly articulate the policies and procedures that will govern the procurement process. Include information on how orders will be placed, payment terms, and any negotiated discounts or incentives.

Specify the quality control measures that will be implemented for procured goods or services. Ensure that suppliers adhere to regulatory requirements, industry standards, and any specific quality benchmarks set by the company.

Identify potential risks in the procurement process, such as supply chain disruptions or changes in market conditions. Develop strategies to mitigate these risks, including alternative sourcing options and contingency plans.

2. Inventory Management

Clearly define inventory policies, including reorder points, order quantities, and lead times. Specify how inventory levels will be monitored and adjusted to prevent stockouts or excess inventory.

Describe the inventory management systems and technology that will be employed. This may include barcode scanning, RFID technology, or specialized software for real-time tracking and data analysis.

Categorize inventory based on factors such as demand, value, and shelf life. This segmentation can aid in prioritizing stock management activities and optimizing storage space.

Detail the methods used for demand forecasting. This could involve historical sales data analysis, market trends, or collaboration with suppliers to ensure that inventory levels align with anticipated demand. If you are writing a business plan for a pre-existing business, your organization should already have this information available. If you are writing a business plan for a new business, you may have to do market research on similar businesses in your area to gather this forecasting data.

3. Distribution Process

Outline the distribution channels that will be utilized to deliver products or services to customers. This may involve direct sales, partnerships with retailers, e-commerce platforms, or a combination of these.

Specify the logistics and transportation methods employed in the distribution process. Address how products will be stored, packed, and shipped, considering factors such as cost-effectiveness and environmental impact. If you are dealing in perishable goods that have a shelf-life you will also need to include that information in this section.

Describe the order fulfillment process, including order processing times, shipping options, and delivery schedules. Consider customer expectations and strive to meet or exceed industry standards for delivery speed and accuracy.

Integrate customer service into the distribution process. Provide information on how customer inquiries, returns, and feedback will be handled, emphasizing a customer-centric approach to post-purchase interactions.

4. Continuous Improvement and Monitoring

Define Key Performance Indicators (KPIs) for procurement, inventory management, and distribution processes. These metrics could include order fulfillment times, inventory turnover rates, and supplier performance evaluations.

Emphasize the importance of continuous monitoring and adaptation. Regularly review processes, collect feedback from stakeholders, and be prepared to make adjustments to enhance efficiency and address emerging challenges.

Detailing the procurement, inventory management, and distribution processes in a business plan involves a comprehensive approach that considers the entire supply chain. By addressing each step with clarity and precision, businesses can build a robust operational foundation that supports growth, efficiency, and customer satisfaction.

Quality Control

Maintaining and monitoring the quality of products or services is a critical aspect of a business plan. This ensures that a company not only meets but consistently exceeds customer expectations, building trust and loyalty.

The following steps outline how to articulate these processes within a business plan:

1. Clearly Define Quality Standards

Begin by clearly defining the quality standards that your products or services must meet. This includes specifications, features, and performance expectations. Ensure that these standards align with industry benchmarks and customer preferences.

2. Establish Quality Control Processes

Outline the specific processes and procedures that will be implemented to maintain quality throughout the production or service delivery lifecycle. This could involve inspections, testing protocols, and adherence to regulatory requirements.

3. Quality Assurance Team

Introduce the quality assurance team responsible for overseeing and implementing quality control measures. Specify their roles and responsibilities, emphasizing their importance in upholding the company's commitment to excellence.

4. Incorporate Quality from the Design Stage

Emphasize that quality is not just an endpoint but is embedded in the design and development phase. Describe how product designers and service developers consider quality aspects from the initial concept through to the final execution.

5. Prototyping and Testing

Explain how prototyping and testing are integral to the development process. This could involve creating prototypes for physical products or conducting trial runs for service delivery to identify and address potential quality issues early on.

6. Select Reliable Suppliers and Vendors

Discuss the criteria for selecting suppliers and vendors, emphasizing their commitment to quality. Clearly state that the company only engages with partners who share the same dedication to delivering high-quality components or services.

7. Supplier Audits and Assessments

Detail how the company conducts regular audits and assessments of suppliers and vendors to ensure they continue to meet quality standards. This could include on-site inspections, performance evaluations, and adherence to contractual quality agreements.

8. Real-time Monitoring Systems

Introduce real-time monitoring systems and technologies that will be employed during the production or service delivery process. Explain how these systems contribute to early detection of any deviations from established quality standards.

9. Quality Metrics and Key Performance Indicators (KPIs)

Define specific quality metrics and key performance indicators that will be tracked. This could include defect rates, customer satisfaction scores, and any other relevant indicators that reflect the quality of products or services.

10. Customer Feedback Mechanisms

Highlight the methods through which the company collects customer feedback on product quality or service satisfaction. This could involve surveys, reviews, or direct communication channels to understand customer perceptions.

11. Post-Service Evaluation

Explain any post-service evaluation processes, especially for service-oriented businesses, to ensure that the quality of service is continuously assessed even after the interaction with the customer.

Another phase of Quality Control involves developing Continuous Improvement Strategies. Steps in this process include:

1. Root Cause Analysis

Discuss how the company will conduct root cause analysis in the event of quality issues. Explain the corrective and preventive actions that will be taken to address identified issues and prevent their recurrence.

2. Continuous Training and Development

Emphasize the commitment to continuous training and development for employees involved in product development or service delivery. This ensures that the team remains updated on quality standards and best practices.

Quality Control also involves compliance with regulatory standards in your chosen industry. For this section of your business plan, be sure to include:

1. Regulatory Compliance Assurance

Address how the company will ensure compliance with industry-specific regulations and standards. This is crucial for industries where regulatory adherence directly impacts product or service quality. Examples might include pharmaceuticals companies, food products, or machinery where safety is important while operating, or any other product or service subject to government regulation.
Steps to include in a business plan to assure regulatory compliance include:

2. Certifications and Audits

Outline any certifications the company holds or plans to achieve to demonstrate its commitment to quality. Describe how regular audits will be conducted to verify ongoing compliance. Neglecting this section of a business plan can be a red flag to investors and other stakeholders.

Detailing how your business will maintain and monitor the quality of its products or services is a vital component of your business plan. By clearly outlining the processes, teams, and technologies involved, you demonstrate to stakeholders and potential investors that your company is committed to delivering consistent and high-quality offerings, ultimately contributing to long-term success and customer satisfaction.

Human Resources

Providing a comprehensive overview of staffing needs in a business plan is crucial for outlining the human resources strategy that will drive the success of the organization. This section should cover various aspects, including roles and responsibilities, hiring strategies, and training programs.

Here's a breakdown of how to effectively present these elements in your business plan:

1. Organizational Structure

Begin by presenting the overall organizational structure of the company. This should have been covered in the Organizational Structure section of the business plan, but if you didn't already do this in the previous section, be sure to define key leadership positions, departmental divisions, and reporting relationships.
Clearly articulate the roles and responsibilities of each position within the organization.

2. Job Descriptions

Again, if you didn't already to this in your Organizational Structure section, be sure to provide detailed job descriptions for key positions. Highlight the skills, qualifications, and experience required for each role.
Emphasize how each role contributes to the overall success of the company and supports the achievement of its strategic objectives.

3. Team Dynamics

Discuss the collaboration and communication dynamics within teams. Be sure to cover how communication channels work among various departments and divisions if you haven't already discussed this elsewhere. Address how cross-functional collaboration will be encouraged in order to foster a cohesive and productive working environment.

Next you will need to include information about your company's hiring strategies. Your employees are the most important part of your organization, so investors and other stakeholders will be particularly interested in this section.
Steps to outline your venture's hiring strategies include:

1. Recruitment Plan

Outline the company's recruitment plan, including the channels and methods that will be utilized to attract top talent. Specify whether the company will rely on in-house recruiters, external agencies, online job boards, or networking events.

2. Selection Criteria

Define the criteria for selecting candidates. Highlight the qualities, skills, and values that the company values in its employees. Discuss how the hiring process aligns with the company's culture and values.

3. Diversity and Inclusion

Address the company's commitment to diversity and inclusion. Discuss strategies for attracting a diverse workforce and creating an inclusive workplace culture.

4. Onboarding Process

Briefly describe the onboarding process for new hires. Explain how the company ensures a smooth transition for employees, providing them with the necessary information, training, and resources to integrate into their roles effectively.

Any business entity is only as successful as its employees. A well-trained staff is a key component to any venture. Any effective business plan should include a section on how you plan to train and develop your work staff.

Steps for the training and development section include:

1. Skills Development

Discuss the company's approach to skills development. Explain how training programs will be designed to enhance the skills and competencies of employees.

Highlight any specific technical or soft skills that are crucial for the success of the business.

2. Continuous Learning Culture

Emphasize the importance of a continuous learning culture within the organization. Discuss ongoing training initiatives, mentorship programs, and opportunities for professional development.

3. Leadership Development

Address leadership development programs for key personnel. Demonstrate how the company invests in developing leadership skills internally to support long-term growth and succession planning. Include selection criteria for those groomed for leadership positions.

4. Performance Management

Describe the performance management system in place, including regular performance reviews, goal-setting processes, and feedback mechanisms.

Explain how performance evaluations contribute to the identification of training needs and career development opportunities. Link this evaluation process back to overall operations and explain specifically how it will enhance your operations.

It doesn't matter how talented and skilled your work staff is if you can't keep them. Employee turnover is a problem that can significantly impact any business's operational strategy. The next section of your human resources overview should include how your organization implements talent retention.

Key elements of any employee retention strategy should include:

1. Employee Benefits and Perks

Briefly outline the employee benefits and perks offered by the company. This could include health insurance, retirement plans, flexible work arrangements, or other incentives.

2. Recognition and Rewards

Discuss the company's approach to recognizing and rewarding employee contributions. Highlight any performance-based incentives or employee recognition programs in place.

3. Career Advancement Opportunities

Emphasize the company's commitment to providing career advancement opportunities. Discuss potential career paths, promotions, and opportunities for employees to grow within the organization.

Providing an overview of staffing needs in your business plan involves detailing the organizational structure, hiring strategies, and training programs that will contribute to the success and sustainability of your business. A well-defined human resources strategy ensures that the right people are in the right roles, equipped with the skills and support necessary to drive the company's objectives forward.

Regulatory Compliance

Addressing legal and regulatory requirements pertinent to your industry is crucial in a business plan for demonstrating a comprehensive understanding of the legal landscape and ensuring compliance.

Here's a guide on how to effectively incorporate this information into your business plan:

1. Industry-Specific Regulations

Identify and provide an overview of the key legal and regulatory requirements specific to your industry. Clearly articulate the compliance standards that your business must adhere to.

2. Local, State, and Federal Laws

Distinguish between local, state, and federal regulations that impact your business. Clearly state how your business plans to comply with each level of regulatory oversight.

The next part of your Operations Plan should demonstrate how you intend to comply with regulations and laws. This section should include:

1. Compliance Team

Introduce the team or individual responsible for overseeing legal and regulatory compliance within the organization. This could be a legal department, compliance officer, or an external legal consultant. At a minimum, you should have an attorney on retainer as a consultant for any compliance issues that might arise during the course of business.

2. Monitoring and Reporting

Detail the processes in place for monitoring changes in laws and regulations relevant to your industry. Explain how your company will stay informed and update its practices accordingly.

3. Regular Audits and Assessments

Describe how your business will conduct regular audits and assessments to ensure ongoing compliance. This could involve internal reviews, external audits, or a combination of both.

There are specific legal requirements and considerations for every type of business. Consider the compliance issues particular to your business, and include your operations plan for addressing each of the following, where pertinent:

1.Intellectual Property Protection

If applicable, outline the steps taken to protect intellectual property (patents, trademarks, copyrights). Address any ongoing efforts to monitor and enforce these protections.

3. Data Privacy and Security

Discuss how your business will handle and protect customer data in compliance with data protection laws. Address privacy policies, consent mechanisms, and cybersecurity measures.

4. Employment Laws

Outline how your business complies with employment laws, including regulations related to wages, working hours, employee benefits, and workplace safety. Address any industry-specific labor standards.

5. Environmental Regulations

If your industry has environmental considerations, detail how your business adheres to environmental regulations. Discuss sustainability initiatives and any measures taken to minimize environmental impact.

Risk management impacts all areas of a business. In the legal compliance section, you will want to identify potential risks specific to regulatory and legal compliance issues.
Steps in this process include:

1. Risk Identification

Identify and discuss potential legal and regulatory risks specific to your industry. This could include changes in legislation, emerging legal trends, or industry-specific challenges.

2. Risk Mitigation Strategies

Outline the strategies in place to mitigate legal and regulatory risks. This might involve contingency plans, legal counsel, or insurance coverage.

An important part of the Operations Plan is the strategy for addressing legal issues when they come up. Most businesses will eventually face some sort of legal challenge. Being prepared and having a strategy for responding to legal challenges when they arise will show investors and other stakeholders that you are detail-oriented and a strategic thinker when it comes to your business's operational details.

Your legal response protocols should include, at a minimum, the following two strategies:

1. Response Protocols

Detail how your business will respond in the event of legal challenges. This could involve having a legal response team, protocols for communication, and engagement with legal counsel.

2. Litigation Preparedness

Discuss the measures in place to ensure your business is prepared for potential litigation. This includes record-keeping practices, documentation of compliance efforts, incident reporting, and strategies for dispute resolution.

Addressing legal and regulatory requirements in your business plan requires a thorough understanding of the legal landscape relevant to your industry. Clearly articulating compliance strategies, risk management, and legal contingency plans demonstrates to stakeholders and potential investors that your business is committed to ethical and lawful practices, fostering trust and sustainability for your venture.

Risk Management

Identifying potential risks and developing effective mitigation strategies are essential components of the operations plan in a business plan. This section helps demonstrate a comprehensive understanding of the challenges the business might face and the proactive measures in place to address these challenges.

While you should have briefly touched on Risk Management in other sections of your business plan, here in the Operations Plan section you will go into much greater detail, since Risk Management will have an effect on every aspect of your business's operations.

Here's a guide on how to integrate risk identification and mitigation strategies into your operations plan.

The first step in managing risk is to identify all potential areas of risk in your business operations. The steps for this include:

1. Comprehensive Risk Assessment

Begin by conducting a thorough risk assessment across all aspects of your operations. Consider financial, operational, strategic, compliance, and external risks that could impact your business.

2. Strengths, Weaknesses, Opportunities, Threats (SWOT) Analysis

Utilize a SWOT (Strengths, Weaknesses, Opportunities, Threats) analysis to identify internal and external factors that may pose risks to your operations. This provides a holistic view of the business environment.

3. Stakeholder Input

Engage with key stakeholders, including employees, suppliers, customers, and industry experts, to gather diverse perspectives on potential risks. These insights can provide valuable information that might be overlooked internally.

4. Historical Data and Industry Trends

Analyze historical data, industry trends, and market conditions to identify patterns or potential risks that may arise. This helps in anticipating challenges based on past occurrences.

5. Categorize Risks

Classify identified risks into different categories, such as financial, operational, legal, market, and technological. This categorization helps in organizing and prioritizing risks for mitigation planning.

6. Likelihood and Impact Assessment

Assess the likelihood and potential impact of each identified risk. This involves evaluating the probability of occurrence and the severity of consequences if the risk materializes.

Once you have a good understanding of risks that might arise during your business operations, the next step is to outline a risk mitigation strategy.

Steps for developing this strategy include:

1. Risk Mitigation Planning

Develop specific mitigation plans for each identified risk. Clearly outline the steps that will be taken to reduce the likelihood of occurrence or minimize the impact if the risk does materialize.

2. Risk Transfer and Insurance

Identify risks that can be transferred to third parties through contracts or insurance. Explain how your business will use insurance coverage or contractual arrangements to mitigate financial and operational risks. Be aware of situations in which contractual obligations might make you liable for the actions of your contractors, and mitigate this risk through contract riders or other means. You may need to consult with an attorney for this.

3. Diversification and Redundancy
Introduce strategies that involve diversification and redundancy. For instance, having multiple suppliers or distribution channels can mitigate the impact of disruptions in a single area of the supply chain.

4. Scenario Planning
Conduct scenario planning exercises to simulate potential risk scenarios. This helps in identifying gaps in your mitigation strategies and refining them for better preparedness.

5. Training and Skill Development:
Mitigate risks related to human factors by investing in training and skill development programs for employees. Well-trained staff can respond more effectively to challenges and prevent operational disruptions.

6. Regular Monitoring and Evaluation
Establish a system for regular monitoring and evaluation of risk mitigation strategies. This involves ongoing assessment of the effectiveness of implemented measures and adjustments based on changing circumstances.

A key component of Risk Management is effective communication. In fact, when a risk endangers a company's operations, it is most often the result of poor or nonexistent communication.

The steps to developing an effective communication strategy include:

1. Internal and External Communication
Develop a communication plan for both internal and external stakeholders. Clearly communicate the identified risks, the mitigation strategies in place, and the roles and responsibilities of key personnel during a risk event.

2 Crisis Management Protocols
Outline crisis management protocols, including communication channels, escalation procedures, and media responses. A well-prepared crisis management plan enhances the ability to respond promptly and effectively to unforeseen events.

3 Contingency Plans

The final part of a risk management strategy is developing contingency plans. Create contingency plans that outline specific actions to be taken if a risk materializes. Contingency plans should be detailed and accessible to relevant personnel to ensure a swift and coordinated response.

Allocate resources, including personnel and finances, for implementing mitigation and contingency plans. This ensures that the necessary tools and expertise are readily available when needed.

Integrating risk identification and mitigation strategies into the Operations Plan of your business plan demonstrates a proactive approach to addressing uncertainties. By presenting a comprehensive understanding of potential risks and showcasing well-thought-out mitigation plans, your business plan becomes a powerful tool for instilling confidence in stakeholders and investors, underlining your commitment to operational resilience and success.

Strategies for Developing an Operations Plan

There are certain overall strategies to keep in mind while developing the Operations Plan section of an effective business plan. These components include:

Collaborative Approach

Involve key stakeholders, including operations managers, department heads, and relevant staff, in the development process. This ensures a comprehensive and realistic plan that considers various perspectives. If this is a new venture and not a pre-existing business, you may need to hir consultants or research similar businesses for this information.

Data-Driven Decision Making

Base your operational strategies on reliable data and market analysis. Use metrics to measure performance, identify areas for improvement, and make informed decisions. This is called *evidence-based planning* because you are relying on metrics that can be measured, quantified, and cross-checked. In other words, you are relying on demonstrable data instead of guesswork.

Flexibility and Adaptability

Acknowledge that business environments are dynamic. Build flexibility into your operations plan to adapt to changing market conditions, technology advancements, and unforeseen challenges.

Continuous Improvement

Integrate a culture of continuous improvement into your Operations Plan. Encourage feedback from employees and customers, and use this information to refine and enhance your processes over time. When you are able to do so, you will have demonstrated to investors and other stakeholders that you are making a conscious effort to make your business the best it can be.

An Operations Plan is a critical component of a comprehensive and effective business plan. It provides a detailed roadmap for how a company will function on a day-to-day basis, ensuring efficiency, effectiveness, and the delivery of value to customers.

By carefully considering the key components and implementing thoughtful strategies, you can create a robust Operations Plan that contributes significantly to your overall success.

9 Financial Plan

A well-crafted financial plan is a necessity for any successful business plan. It serves as a guide for managing resources, making informed decisions, and achieving long-term financial sustainability. In this chapter, we will delve into the essential components and considerations involved in creating a robust financial plan for a business.

Begin your financial plan with a concise executive summary that provides an overview of your business's financial health and objectives. Highlight key financial goals, such as revenue targets, profit margins, and expense management strategies. This section should be included in the Executive Summary outlined in Chapter 2, but it wouldn't hurt to reiterate the main points at the beginning of the Financial Plan section of your business plan.

There are multiple elements you should consider in your Financial Plan to be able to attract serious investors. Some of these are:

Sales Forecast
The sales forecast is a fundamental element of the Financial Plan. It involves estimating future sales based on market research, historical data, and industry trends. A realistic sales forecast forms the basis for projecting revenue and sets the tone for the entire Financial Plan section of your business plan. When presenting your business plan to investors, they will scrutinize this section in particular to assess whether your business is worthy of investing in.

Writing a sales forecast for a business plan involves estimating future sales based on various factors and considerations. A well-thought-out sales forecast provides a foundation for other financial projections in your business plan and demonstrates your understanding of market dynamics.

Begin by conducting thorough market research. Understand your target audience, their needs, and the overall market conditions. Analyze industry trends, competition, and potential market growth. This information will help you make informed assumptions about your sales potential.

Next, clearly outline the channels through which you plan to sell your products or services. Whether it's through direct sales, online platforms, partnerships, or distribution channels, each channel may have different dynamics that affect your sales forecast.

If applicable, segment your market. Different customer segments may have distinct purchasing behaviors. Tailoring your sales forecast to these segments provides a more accurate prediction of potential sales.

Estimate the number of units of products or services you expect to sell. Be realistic and consider factors such as market demand, seasonality, and economic conditions. Don't yield to the temptation to paint a rosy picture. Be realistic, as investors who are savvy will know what you're doing if you attempt to exaggerate sales potential.

Set realistic pricing based on your costs, competitor pricing, and perceived value. Pricing decisions will directly impact your revenue projections.

Determine a reasonable sales growth rate. This could be a percentage increase over time based on your market research and the growth trajectory of similar businesses.

Factor in any specific marketing or sales strategies you plan to implement to drive growth.

Understand the typical sales cycle for your industry. Consider the time it takes from lead generation to closing a sale. This is especially important for businesses with longer sales cycles, such as those in business-to-business markets.

Take into account any seasonality or trends that may affect your sales. For example, retail businesses may experience higher sales during holiday seasons, while other industries may have specific peak periods.

If applicable, analyze your sales pipeline. Track potential leads and their progression through the sales process. This can provide insights into the conversion rates at different stages of the sales funnel.

Consider external factors that may influence your sales forecast, such as economic conditions, changes in consumer behavior, or industry regulations. Acknowledging these factors adds credibility to your projections.

Clearly document the assumptions you've made in creating your sales forecast. This includes the reasoning behind your estimates, the data sources used, and any external factors considered. Investors and stakeholders will appreciate transparency and a well-supported forecast.

Remember also that a sales forecast is not a static document. Regularly review and update it based on actual performance, market changes, and feedback. Adjust your forecast as needed to ensure it remains accurate and aligned with your business goals.

By following these steps, you can create a comprehensive and realistic sales forecast that forms a solid foundation for your business plan. Remember that accuracy and transparency are key when presenting your sales forecast to potential investors or lenders.

Identify and categorize your business's expenses, including fixed costs (rent, salaries) and variable costs (utilities, raw materials). Accurate expense projections enable you to calculate your break-even point and determine the amount of revenue needed to cover costs.

Cash Flow Statement

Creating a cash flow statement for a business plan is crucial for understanding the movement of cash in and out of your business. It provides valuable insights into your business's liquidity, helps identify potential cash shortages, and guides financial decision-making.

Here's a step-by-step guide on how to write a cash flow statement for your business plan:

Understand the Components

A cash flow statement is divided into three main sections: *operating activities*, *investing activities*, and *financing activities*.

Operating activities include cash transactions related to your primary business operations.

Investing activities cover cash transactions for purchasing or selling assets.

Financing activities involve cash transactions with the business's owners, lenders, or investors.

Operating Activities

Start with the operating activities section. List all cash inflows and outflows related to your core business operations.

Include cash received from customers, payments to suppliers, employee salaries, and any other operating expenses.

Calculate the net cash flow from operating activities by subtracting cash outflows from cash inflows.

Investing Activities

Move on to the investing activities section. Include cash transactions related to buying or selling assets.

Examples of investing activities include purchasing equipment, selling property, or acquiring other businesses.

Calculate the net cash flow from investing activities by subtracting cash outflows from cash inflows.

Financing Activities

Proceed to the financing activities section. Include cash transactions with owners, lenders, or investors.

Common financing activities include receiving loans, repaying debt, issuing or repurchasing shares, and distributing dividends.

Calculate the net cash flow from financing activities by subtracting cash outflows from cash inflows.

Net Cash Flow

Sum the net cash flows from operating, investing, and financing activities to determine the overall net cash flow.

Positive net cash flow indicates more cash coming into the business than going out, while negative net cash flow signals potential liquidity challenges.

Beginning and Ending Cash Balance

Specify the beginning cash balance, which is the amount of cash your business has at the start of the period covered by the statement.

Add the net cash flow to the beginning cash balance to calculate the ending cash balance.

Formatting

Present the cash flow statement in a clear and organized format. Use tables or charts to enhance readability. Consider using categories and subtotals for each section to provide a detailed breakdown of cash inflows and outflows.

Document Assumptions

Clearly document any assumptions made in preparing the cash flow statement. This includes assumptions about payment terms, collection periods, and other factors that influence cash flow.

Regular Review and Update

A cash flow statement is a dynamic document that should be regularly reviewed and updated. This is especially important when there are changes in business operations, market conditions, or financial strategies. At a bare minimum it should be updated quarterly. Update more frequently depending on your cash flow situation as circumstances dictate.

Interpret the Results

Analyze the results of the cash flow statement. Identify trends, assess the business's ability to meet short-term obligations, and evaluate the impact of financing and investment decisions on cash flow.

By following these steps, you can create a comprehensive cash flow statement that provides a clear picture of your business's cash position. This document is invaluable for decision-making, financial planning, and presenting a well-rounded business plan to potential investors or lenders.

Profit and Loss Statement

A Profit and Loss (P&L) statement, also known as an Income Statement, is a financial document that summarizes the revenue, costs, and expenses incurred by a business during a specific period. Crafting a P&L statement is essential for your business plan as it provides a snapshot of your company's profitability. You won't be able to attract investors or lenders without a well-written P&L statement.

Here is a step-by-step guide on how to write a Profit and Loss statement for your business plan:

Understand the Structure

A P&L statement typically consists of three main sections: *revenue, cost of goods sold (COGS)*, and *operating expenses.*

Revenue represents the total income generated from sales.

Cost of Goods Sold (COGS) includes the direct costs associated with producing goods or services.

Operating expenses encompass all other costs related to running the business.

Revenue

Start with the revenue section. Detail each revenue stream separately, such as product sales, service fees, or other income sources.

Be clear about your pricing strategy and the volume of sales expected for each product or service.

Calculate the total revenue by summing up the individual revenue streams.

Cost of Goods Sold (COGS)

Move on to the COGS section. List the direct costs associated with producing goods or services.

For product-based businesses, COGS may include raw materials, manufacturing labor, and production costs.
For service-based businesses, COGS may be less direct but could include labor costs directly tied to service delivery.
Subtract COGS from total revenue to calculate gross profit.

Gross Profit

Gross profit is a key indicator of your business's profitability before accounting for operating expenses. It is calculated by subtracting COGS from total revenue.

Operating Expenses

List and categorize all operating expenses. This includes items like rent, utilities, salaries, marketing expenses, and other overhead costs.
Operating expenses are typically broken down into categories such as selling, general and administrative expenses (SG&A).
Calculate the total operating expenses by summing up the individual categories.

Operating Income

Subtract total operating expenses from gross profit to calculate operating income.
Operating income reflects the profitability of your core business operations.

Other Income and Expenses

Include any other income or expenses not covered in the main sections. This could involve interest income, interest expenses, or one-time gains or losses.
Adjust operating income by adding or subtracting these items to calculate net income before taxes.

Taxes

Deduct applicable taxes from net income before taxes to calculate net income after taxes.
Clearly specify the tax rate used in your calculations.

Net Income

Net income represents the bottom line - the overall profit or loss your business incurred during the specified period.
This is calculated by subtracting taxes from net income before taxes.

Formatting

Present the P&L statement in a clear and organized format. Use tables or charts to enhance readability.
Consider using percentages to analyze the proportion of expenses to revenue.

Document Assumptions

Clearly document any assumptions made in preparing the P&L statement. This includes assumptions about sales growth, cost structures, and other financial factors.

Regular Review and Update

A P&L statement is not a static document. Regularly review and update it based on actual financial performance, market changes, and business strategies. Again, update quarterly at a bare minimum, or at any time when there is a substantial change in P&L.

By following these steps, you can create a comprehensive Profit and Loss statement that provides a detailed overview of your business's financial performance. This document is crucial for assessing profitability, making informed financial decisions, and presenting a thorough business plan to potential investors or lenders.

Balance Sheet

A *Balance Sheet* is a financial statement that provides a snapshot of your business's financial position at a specific point in time. It is a key component of a business plan, offering insights into a company's assets, liabilities, and equity.
Here is a step-by-step guide on how to write a Balance Sheet section for your business plan:

Understand the Components

A Balance Sheet is divided into three main sections: *assets*, *liabilities*, and *equity*.
Assets are what the business owns and can include current assets (e.g., cash, inventory) and non-current assets (e.g., property, equipment).
Liabilities represent the business's obligations, including current liabilities (e.g., accounts payable) and non-current liabilities (e.g., long-term debt).
Equity is the residual interest in the assets of the business after deducting liabilities.

List Current Assets
Start with current assets, which are assets expected to be converted into cash or used up within one year.
Include items such as cash, accounts receivable, inventory, and other short-term investments.
Sum up the total current assets.

List Non-Current Assets
Proceed to non-current assets, which are long-term assets not expected to be converted into cash within one year.
Include items like property, equipment, intangible assets, and long-term investments.
Sum up the total non-current assets.

Calculate Total Assets
Add the total current assets to the total non-current assets to calculate the overall total assets.

List Current Liabilities
Move on to current liabilities, which are obligations due within one year.
Include items such as accounts payable, short-term debt, and accrued expenses.
Sum up the total current liabilities.

List Non-Current Liabilities
Proceed to non-current liabilities, which are long-term obligations not due within one year.
Include items like long-term debt and deferred tax liabilities.
Sum up the total non-current liabilities.

Calculate Total Liabilities
Add the total current liabilities to the total non-current liabilities to calculate the overall total liabilities.

Calculate Equity
Equity represents the ownership interest in the business. Include items such as common stock, retained earnings, and additional paid-in capital.
Calculate equity by subtracting total liabilities from total assets.

Verify the Balance
Ensure that the equation Assets = Liabilities + Equity holds true.

This confirms the balance and accuracy of your Balance Sheet.

Formatting
Present the Balance Sheet in a clear and organized format. Use tables or charts to enhance readability.
Consider presenting comparative Balance Sheets if applicable (e.g., for multiple periods).

Document Assumptions
Clearly document any assumptions made in preparing the Balance Sheet. This includes assumptions about asset valuations, liabilities, and equity structures.

Regular Review and Update
Like all of your other financial documents, a Balance Sheet is not a static document. Regularly review and update it based on changes in financial positions, business activities, and strategic decisions.

By following these steps, you can create a comprehensive Balance Sheet section for your business plan. A well-prepared Balance Sheet provides a snapshot of your business's financial health and is crucial for understanding the overall financial position of the company.

Risk Assessment
A risk assessment in the financial plan section of a business plan is essential for identifying, analyzing, and mitigating potential risks that could impact the financial stability and success of your business.
Here is a step-by-step guide on how to write a risk assessment in the financial plan:

Identify Potential Risks
Begin by identifying potential risks that could affect your business. These risks may include market fluctuations, economic downturns, competition, regulatory changes, technological disruptions, and more.
Categorize risks into external and internal factors to provide a comprehensive overview.

Assess the Impact
Evaluate the potential impact of each identified risk on your business's financial performance. Consider both the short-term and long-term consequences.
Quantify the potential financial loss or impact on revenue, expenses,

and overall profitability.

Determine the Likelihood

Assess the likelihood of each identified risk occurring. Use historical data, market research, and expert opinions to gauge the probability of each risk materializing.

Consider external factors that may increase or decrease the likelihood of certain risks.

Prioritize Risks

Prioritize risks based on their potential impact and likelihood. Focus on high-impact, high-likelihood risks first, but don't neglect those with lower probability that could still have significant consequences.

Mitigation Strategies

Develop strategies to mitigate or manage each identified risk. This could involve implementing preventive measures, creating contingency plans, or purchasing insurance.

Specify actions, policies, or procedures that will be put in place to reduce the likelihood or impact of each risk.

Financial Contingency Planning

Outline specific financial contingency plans for high-impact risks. This may include setting aside reserves, establishing lines of credit, or diversifying revenue streams.

Clearly state how these contingency plans would be activated in response to identified risks.

Scenario Analysis

Conduct scenario analysis to understand how your financials would be affected under different risk scenarios. This involves modeling the financial impact of various risk combinations and assessing their cumulative effect.

Sensitivity Analysis

Perform sensitivity analysis to evaluate how changes in key financial variables (such as sales, expenses, interest rates) would impact your financial projections under different risk scenarios.

Documentation and Transparency

Clearly document your risk assessment process, including the identified risks, their impact and likelihood assessments, and the corresponding mitigation strategies.

Transparency is crucial when presenting this information to stakeholders, as it instills confidence and demonstrates that you've thoroughly considered potential challenges.

Regular Review and Update

Risks are dynamic and can change over time. Regularly review and update your risk assessment as market conditions, regulations, and other external factors evolve.
Periodic reviews ensure that your risk mitigation strategies remain relevant and effective.

Communication

Communicate your risk assessment findings and mitigation strategies clearly in the financial plan section of your business plan. This is particularly important when presenting your plan to potential investors, lenders, or partners.

By incorporating a comprehensive risk assessment into your financial plan, you demonstrate a proactive approach to managing uncertainties and increase the credibility of your business plan. It also helps you prepare for potential challenges, making your business more resilient in the face of unforeseen events.

Funding Needs

The Funding Needs section in the financial plan of a business plan is crucial for conveying to investors, lenders, or stakeholders the amount of capital required to start or grow the business. It provides insights into how the funds will be utilized and why the requested amount is necessary.
Here is a step-by-step guide on how to write a Funding Needs section:

Determine the Purpose of Funds

Clearly define the purpose for which you need funding. Whether it's for startup costs, working capital, expansion, research and development, marketing, or other specific needs, be explicit about how the funds will be allocated.

Breakdown of Funding Uses

Provide a detailed breakdown of how the funds will be used. Categorize the uses into specific areas, such as equipment purchase, marketing campaigns, hiring, technology investments, and any other relevant categories.

Justify Funding Amount

Clearly justify the requested funding amount. Base your figures on thorough research, market analysis, and realistic projections. Demonstrate a clear understanding of your business's financial needs and the factors influencing them.

Timeline for Fund Utilization

Outline the timeline for utilizing the funds. Specify when and how the funds will be disbursed and how they align with your business milestones and growth plans.

Quantify Working Capital Requirements

If applicable, quantify your working capital requirements. This includes funds needed to cover day-to-day operational expenses, such as inventory, accounts payable, and employee salaries. Provide a clear calculation to support your figures.

Show Expected ROI

Explain how the infusion of funds will contribute to the growth and profitability of the business. Illustrate the expected return on investment (ROI) and how the funding will positively impact the financial performance of the company.

Risk Assessment and Mitigation

Acknowledge any potential risks associated with your funding needs. Demonstrate that you've considered the risks and outline mitigation strategies. This exhibits a realistic and thoughtful approach to potential challenges.

Alternative Funding Sources

Mention any alternative funding sources you've explored or intend to explore. This could include personal investment, loans, grants, partnerships, or other financing options. Highlighting multiple avenues shows flexibility and resourcefulness.

Terms and Conditions

If you're seeking external funding, clearly state the terms and conditions you are proposing. This includes the amount of equity or debt you are willing to offer, interest rates, repayment terms, and any other relevant terms.

Financial Projections

Support your funding needs with relevant financial projections. Provide a forecast of your income statement, cash flow statement, and balance sheet, showing how the funding will impact your financial performance over time.

Exit Strategy (if applicable)

If you are seeking equity financing, briefly discuss your exit strategy. This outlines how investors will eventually recoup their investment, whether through an IPO, acquisition, or other means.

Documentation

Back up your funding needs with detailed documentation, such as quotes, estimates, market research, and any other relevant supporting materials.

Professional Presentation

Present your funding needs in a professional and organized manner. Use clear and concise language, and make use of visuals like tables or charts to enhance understanding.

Executive Summary

Summarize the key points of your funding needs in the executive summary of your business plan. This provides a quick overview for busy investors or stakeholders.

By following these steps, you can create a comprehensive Funding Needs section in your financial plan that clearly communicates the purpose, amount, and justification for the funds you are seeking. This section is critical for instilling confidence in potential investors or lenders and for demonstrating your strategic approach to financial management.

A financial plan is a dynamic document that should be regularly reviewed and updated. Establish a schedule for financial reviews, and be prepared to adapt your plan based on changing market conditions, business performance, and strategic goals.

By addressing key components such as sales forecasts, expense management, cash flow, and risk assessment, you lay the foundation for informed decision-making and financial stability. Regularly revisiting and adjusting your financial plan allows your business to stay resilient in the face of challenges.

10 Risk Analysis

Writing a comprehensive risk analysis for a business plan is essential for identifying potential threats and uncertainties that could impact the success of your business.

In this chapter we'll be reviewing step-by-step guide to help you create a thorough risk analysis. Some of the information for writing a risk analysis has already been reviewed for other sections.

For example, when writing the Financial Plan section, you will want to include elements of risk analysis pertinent to the financial planning for your organization. You may also choose to include that information in this section, or just save all information pertaining to risk analysis for when you write the Risk Analysis section of your business plan. Where the information is included is less important than making sure it's included somewhere in your business plan.

The steps for writing a comprehensive Risk Analysis section are outlined below.

Identify Risks
Before you can mitigate risks, you must first know what those risks are. There are two basic types of risk that can impact your business: Internal and external risks.

Internal Risk Assessment
Internal risks in a business plan refer to factors within the organization that may pose a threat to its successful operation and achievement of objectives. Identifying internal risks is a critical step in risk assessment, as it allows the business to proactively manage and mitigate potential issues.

Here is a guide on how to identify internal risks for risk assessment in a business plan:

Operational Risks
Operational risks are those risks associated with day-to-day operations and processes. For this section, first assess the efficiency of production processes. Next, examine the reliability of equipment and technology. Evaluate the effectiveness of supply chain management. Will you always be able to get the goods you need when you need them? Are there alternative suppliers?
Finally, consider the adequacy of inventory management. Will you always have inventory on hand when needed? What contributes to inventory shortages or overstocks? How can those risks be mitigated?

Financial Risks
Financial risks are those risks related to financial management and resources. Begin by reviewing cash flow projections and financial statements. Assess the level of debt and its impact on financial stability. Evaluate the dependence on a specific revenue stream. Is diversification possible? If so, how?
Consider your business's exposure to currency fluctuations. What is your long-term strategy for risk management when the market is slow?

Human Resources Risks
Human resources risks are those risks associated with the workforce and organizational structure. Begin this section by assessing the skills and competencies of employees. Consider the impact of turnover, especially key personnel. Consider the ways in which employee turnover can be mitigated, including salaries, bonuses, benefits, and training.
Next, evaluate the effectiveness of employee training and development programs.
Identify potential labor disputes or issues related to job satisfaction, employee safety, and any other factor that might contribute to employee satisfaction.

Technological Risks
Technological risks are those risks related to the use of and reliance on technology. This risk area can be crucial to businesses that rely heavily on the latest technology or the latest software.
For this section, first assess the security of information systems.

Next, evaluate the adequacy of your IT infrastructure. Consider the potential for technology disruptions or failures.

Finally, evaluate your organization's cybersecurity measures. Invest in security as needed, and explain this in your risk management strategy.

Compliance and Legal Risks

Compliance and legal risks are those risks associated with legal and regulatory compliance.

To begin this section, first review current compliance with industry regulations for your organization.

Assess potential changes in laws affecting your business. Identify any pending legal disputes or liabilities.

Next, evaluate the effectiveness of internal controls. Do you have a legal team? Do you need one?

Strategic Risks

Strategic risks are those risks related to you organization's strategic decisions and objectives.

For this section, first assess the market positioning and competitive landscape for your venture.

Next, evaluate the effectiveness of the business model.

Consider the impact changes in consumer behavior might have on your business. For example, Blockbuster was a worldwide chain until video streaming made renting videos obsolete.

Finally, identify potential disruptions in the industry.

Reputational Risks

Reputational risks are those risks related to your organization's public image and brand.

Start this section by first assessing customer satisfaction and feedback. A key element of risk management is collecting regular feedback from your customer base. In this section, explain your company's procedure for collecting and evaluating such data.

Monitor social media and public relations channels for feedback both positive and negative. Have a strategy in place to deal with both types.

Identify potential issues that may harm your company's reputation. Implement a strategy for dealing with such issues as they arise. Also consider preventative measures to keep such issues from arising in the first place.

Supply Chain Risks

Supply chain risks are those risks associated with the supply and distribution of goods and services. These include both the products your company makes, and the raw materials needed to manufacture those goods.

First, evaluate the stability of your suppliers. Assess your venture's vulnerability to supply chain disruptions. Can you get the raw materials you need? Do you have multiple supply chains? If you only have one supply chain, is there a contingency plan should that chain be disrupted?

Finally, identify dependencies on key suppliers or partners. What can be done should those key streams be interrupted or eliminated completely?

Cultural and Organizational Risks

Cultural and organizational risks are those risks related to the organizational culture and structure of your venture. This is a key element of mitigating risk. If your organization's culture promotes an environment where the regular course of business is in danger, it should be dealt with immediately.

First assess the alignment of organizational values with employee behavior. What is employee morale like in your business? Do your employees share your company's vision?

Evaluate the effectiveness of communication within the organization. How good are your communication channels? What can be done to improve them?

Finally, identify potential resistance to change. The only constant is change. This is especially true in the business world. Assess whether your employees are able and willing to adapt and survive the necessary changes required to keep your business a viable entity.

Data Security and Privacy Risks

Data security and privacy risks are those risks associated with the protection of sensitive data.

Secure data is an essential for any business. To write this section of your business plan, first assess the security measures your organization has in place to protect customer data.

Next, evaluate your venture's compliance with data protection regulations and with best standards and practices regarding data security and privacy.

Identify vulnerabilities in data storage and transmission. Develop strategies to deal with breaches or other problematic areas, and discuss these strategies in this section of your business plan.

Facility and Infrastructure Risks

Facility and infrastructure risks are those risks related to the physical facilities and infrastructure of your business.

Begin this section by first assessing the condition of buildings and equipment owned by your organization.

Identify potential risks related to natural disasters or accidents, routine maintenance, or any other factors that could damage or destroy your facilities or the supporting infrastructure.

Finally, evaluate the effectiveness of safety protocols. Does your organization have strategies in place to deal with natural disasters or other unforeseen circumstances that could damage the physical property or infrastructure of your organization? If so, list those strategies and explain them in this section.

Management Risks

Management risks are those risks related to leadership and decision-making within your company.

The first step in writing this section is to evaluate the competency of your management team.

Next, assess the effectiveness of decision-making processes. Do the decisions being made by your management team reflect the goals and values of your company? Are decisions being made by your management team achieving the results you desire?

What is your company's process for evaluating and reviewing employees? Describe your employee evaluation process in this section and describe how it can be used to mitigate risk.

Finally, identify succession planning and key person dependencies. How vulnerable is your organization to losing key leadership? What is your mitigation strategy should this occur?

Employee Health and Safety Risks

These are risks related to the health and safety of employees.

Begin this section by assessing your organization's compliance with occupational health and safety regulations.

Identify potential risks related to workplace accidents or illnesses.

Evaluate the effectiveness of safety training programs. Create risk mitigation pertaining to employee safety and health. This might include regular safety meetings, creating a safety team, or mandatory employee health and safety training.

Environmental Risks

These are risks related to the environmental impact of your business and sustainability of your business's infrastructure and facilities.

Start this section by assessing the environmental impact of your business operations.

Identify potential risks to your business or operations related to changes in environmental regulations. Plan for long-term sustainability.

Evaluate the effectiveness of your company's sustainability initiatives. Implement a strategy of continuous improvement regarding your company's commitment to environmental issues and sustainability, and describe it in this section of your business plan.

Customer and Market Risks

These are risks related to changes in customer preferences and market conditions.

Make sure your organization has methods in place to monitor trends in customer behavior and preferences. Describe that procedure in this section.

Next, assess the potential impact of new competitors or market shifts. What is your company's strategy for dealing with new competitors?

Finally, identify your company's dependencies on a specific customer or market segment. Is it possible to increase the market segments for your goods or services? If so, outline the plan for doing so in this section.

Training and Development Risks

These are risks related to employee skill gaps and deficiencies in your company's training programs.

The first obvious step here is to assess the adequacy of training programs. Do they meet your venture's goals? Do your employees have the skills and knowledge necessary to do their jobs well?

Part of this assessment includes identifying key skills required for business operations.

Finally, evaluate the impact of technological advancements on employee skills. Will some jobs be obsolete in the future as technologies like artificial intelligence and robotics become more commonplace in your industry? What is your risk mitigation strategy if this occurs?

Supply and Demand Risks

These are risks related to fluctuations in supply and demand for products or services.

Start this section by assessing the balance between production capacity and market demand.

Next, identify potential disruptions in the supply chain. Mitigate risk in this area by having multiple suppliers and multiple supply chains if possible.

Finally, evaluate your company's responsiveness to changes in customer demand. Are there any areas of improvement? What are your venture's long-term strategies for constant improvement of supply and demand for your products and services?

Financial Control Risks

These are risks related to financial control and management or your organization.

To start this section, first assess the effectiveness of your company's internal financial controls.

Identify potential fraud or financial mismanagement risks.

Evaluate the accuracy and reliability of financial reporting. Develop risk mitigation strategies should there be any potential for misuse or abuse of company funds, and describe these measures in this section.

Product and Service Quality Risks

These are risks related to the quality and performance of products or services.

A crucial step in risk management in this area is to constantly monitor customer feedback and complaints. In this section, describe your company's procedures for soliciting customer feedback and dealing with complaints.

Next, assess the effectiveness of your company's quality control measures.

Finally, identify potential risks related to product recalls or defects. What is your policy should this occur? Describe it in this section.

Communication Risks

These are risks related to internal and external communication processes for your organization.

Assess the effectiveness of your venture's internal communication channels. Identify potential risks related to miscommunication with stakeholders.

Evaluate the impact of social media and public relations on communication.

Finally, list your risk mitigation strategies for dealing with miscommunications when they occur, and for preventing them before they occur.

External Risk Assessment

External risks in a business plan refer to factors outside the control of the organization that may have an impact on its operations, performance, and success. Identifying external risks is crucial for a comprehensive risk assessment, as it enables businesses to anticipate and proactively address potential challenges.

Here is a guide on how to identify external risks for risk assessment in a business plan:

Market Risks

These are risks associated with changes in the market environment.

To write this section of your business plan, first analyze market trends and demand for products or services.

Next, assess the competitive landscape and potential entry of new competitors.

Identify potential changes in consumer preferences. Market research will help in this area, especially by identifying market trends.

Consider the impact of global market trends and create risk mitigation strategies to deal with these changes as the occur.

Economic Risks

These are risks related to economic conditions and fluctuations.

Monitor macroeconomic indicators (e.g., GDP, inflation rates) and incorporate these into your risk mitigation strategies, then describe them here..

Assess the impact of economic cycles on consumer spending and predict how these might impact your venture. List your strategies for dealing with these eventualities in this section of your business plan..

Identify potential changes in interest rates and exchange rates and discuss how these might impact your business.

Evaluate the overall economic stability of the region in which your business operates.

Political and Regulatory Risks

These are risks associated with changes in political or regulatory environments.

Monitor political stability in the regions in which your venture does business.

Assess potential changes in government policies and regulations.

Identify geopolitical risks and trade restrictions.

Evaluate compliance with industry-specific regulations and develop a strategy that allows your venture to remain compliant.

Technological Risks

These are risks related to technological advancements and disruptions.

Assess the impact of rapid technological changes in your chosen industry.

Identify potential disruptions caused by emerging technologies and develop risk mitigation strategies specific to your industry..

Evaluate cybersecurity threats and vulnerabilities.

Monitor advancements that may render your current technologies obsolete.

Environmental Risks

These are risks associated with environmental factors and sustainability.

Assess the impact of environmental regulations on your business operations.

Identify vulnerabilities to natural disasters or climate change. This can be especially difficult as weather patterns and fire and flood seasons are in fluctuation all over the world.

Evaluate the effectiveness of your company's sustainability initiatives.

Consider reputational risks associated with environmental practices. More and more consumers are becoming aware of and doing business with companies that are committed to sustainable business practices.

Social and Cultural Risks

These are risks related to societal and cultural changes.

Analyze demographic trends and changes in population that might impact your business.

Identify shifts in consumer attitudes and behaviors, specifically related to areas where you do business and issues that might impact how you do business.

Assess the impact of cultural factors on product/service acceptance.

Consider social trends that may affect your business. Describe your mitigation strategies for dealing with these issues in this section of your business plan.

Supplier and Partner Risks

These are risks associated with dependencies on suppliers and partners.

Assess the reliability and stability of key suppliers for your industry.

Identify potential disruptions in the supply chain.

Evaluate the financial health of strategic partners, especially where the supply chain is concerned.

Monitor changes in the business environment of key partners, and create risk mitigation strategies should you lose one or more of those partners. List those strategies in your business plan.

Global Risks

These are risks related to global events and geopolitical dynamics.

Monitor geopolitical tensions and conflicts. Pay special attention to any that might impact your business. This is especially true in today's global economy, even if you have a local business. The recent pandemic demonstrated how global conditions can impact even local businesses.

Assess the impact of global economic conditions as they relate to your ability to operate.

Identify risks associated with international trade and tariffs, especially if they directly impact your supply chain.

Evaluate the potential for currency fluctuations.

Consider all of these global risks and come up with mitigation strategies for each of these, then list them in this section of your business plan.

Legal Risks

These are risks related to legal challenges and liabilities as they pertain to activities that are external to your venture but that still impact your business operations.

Assess compliance with local and international laws and identify potential legal disputes or regulatory fines.

Evaluate the impact of changes in legislation on your business. This means keeping abreast of changes in regulations that might impact you. You may wish to hire legal consultants for this purpose.

Consider risks related to intellectual property and patents.

Create risk mitigation strategies for all of these potential legal risks and itemize them in this section of your business plan.

Health and Pandemic Risks

These are risks associated with public health crises and pandemics.

Assess the potential impact of infectious diseases on operations. If you have retail or other spaces where employees or the public interact, come up with policies that insure the safety of all employees regarding wearing masks or other protective equipment, vaccinations, and what to do if an employee or customer is contagious. Consult with your legal team or an attorney if necessary.

Identify vulnerabilities in the supply chain due to global health events. The recent pandemic demonstrated how important these issues are and how they can impact the day-to-day functioning of a business.

Evaluate the effectiveness of crisis management and contingency plans. Create strategies for all of these possible occurrences and itemize them in this section of the business plan.

Natural Disaster Risks

These are risks related to natural disasters such as earthquakes, hurricanes, or floods.

Assess the susceptibility of your business locations to natural disasters such as floods, fires, or storms.

Identify potential disruptions in operations caused by extreme weather events such as hurricanes, tornados, or earthquakes.

Evaluate the effectiveness of disaster recovery and business continuity plans. Itemize and describe your risk mitigation strategies regarding natural disasters in this section of your business plan.

Competition Risks

These are risks associated with increased competition in the market. Assess the competitive landscape and the potential entry of new competitors.

Identify potential changes in pricing strategies by competitors. How might "price wars" impact your business operations?

Evaluate the impact of mergers and acquisitions in the industry. Outline how this might impact your business operations.

Steps to Identify External Risks

There are several components to consider when identifying external risks to your business. Some of these include:

Environmental Scanning

Regularly monitor external factors that may impact the business.

SWOT Analysis

Conduct a SWOT analysis for your business and its operations. SWOT stands for Strengths, Weaknesses, Opportunities, and Threats. Consider SWOT in the context of potential external threats to your venture.

Industry Analysis

Research and analyze industry trends, benchmarks, and forecasts for your chosen industry and include them in your risk management strategy.

Competitor Analysis
Evaluate the strategies and actions of competitors in the market and include them in your external risk management strategy.

Regulatory Compliance Check
Regularly review and stay compliant with relevant laws and regulations.

Global and Macro-Economic Analysis
Stay informed about global economic conditions and geopolitical events market and include them in your external risk management strategy.

Customer Feedback and Market Research
Gather customer feedback and conduct market research to understand external perceptions and include them in your external risk management strategy.

Scenario Planning
Develop scenarios to anticipate potential external challenges and their impacts and include them in your external risk management strategy.

Networking and Industry Associations
Engage with industry associations and networks to stay informed about external developments.

Consulting Experts
Seek advice from industry experts and consultants to gain insights into external risks.

Identifying and understanding external risks is essential for developing effective risk management strategies in a business plan. Take a proactive approach for long-term success.

Steps to Managing Risks
There are several steps your company should take to identify both internal and external risks prior to completing this section of your business plan.

These steps include:

1. Conduct Internal Audits

Review your company's internal processes, financial records, and systems.

2. Engage Employees

Gather input from employees at all levels to identify potential risks.

3. Review Historical Data

Analyze past incidents or issues to identify recurring patterns. For new companies, assess potential risks by reviewing historical data for companies similar to yours already existing in the market.

4. Use Risk Assessment Tools

Implement risk assessment tools and methodologies outlined in this chapter, or create your own. It may help to consult with similar businesses in your market segment.

5. Benchmarking

Compare internal processes and performance with industry benchmarks. This may require extensive market research, or you may also wish to hire a consulting firm for this information.

6. Categorize Risks

Group risks into categories for better organization (e.g., financial, operational, strategic).
Prioritize risks based on their potential impact and likelihood. You may wish to list risks in order of importance when writing this section of your business plan.

7. Assess Impact and Likelihood

Evaluate the potential impact of each identified risk on your business.
Assess the likelihood of each risk occurring.
Use a scoring system (e.g., low, medium, high, or assign percentages) to quantify impact and likelihood. Explain how each was quantified, and why.

8. Risk Matrix

Create a risk matrix by plotting the impact against the likelihood.
Classify risks into high, medium, and low priority based on the matrix.

9. Risk Mitigation Strategies

Develop strategies to mitigate or reduce the impact of high-priority risks. While it's a good idea to have mitigation strategies for all potential risks, you should pay particular attention to the ones with the higher likelihood.

Include preventive measures and contingency plans and describe those in this section of your business plan.

Consider risk transfer options such as insurance or third party contracts.

10. Monitoring and Review

Outline a plan for regularly reviewing and updating the risk analysis.

Specify who will be responsible for monitoring risks and implementing mitigation strategies.

11. Scenario Analysis

Conduct scenario analysis for critical risks.

Explore best and worst-case scenarios to understand potential outcomes.

Develop strategies for dealing with all foreseeable risks and describe them and how they will be implemented in this section.

12. Document Assumptions

Clearly state any assumptions made during the risk analysis.

Regularly (quarterly at a bare minimum) revisit and update assumptions as the business environment changes.

13. Communication Plan

Define how risks will be communicated within the organization.

Identify key stakeholders and establish communication channels for risk updates.

14. Contingency Budget

Allocate a contingency budget to address unexpected costs associated with risk mitigation.

15. Include in Business Plan

Integrate the risk analysis findings into the business plan.

Provide a summary of key risks, mitigation strategies, and contingency plans.

16. Seek Expert Advice
Consult with industry experts, advisors, or consultants to enhance the depth of your risk analysis.

17. Regulatory Compliance
Ensure that your risk analysis addresses compliance with relevant laws and regulations for both internal and external risks.

18. Review and Update Regularly
Regularly review and update the risk analysis to reflect changes in the business environment.

A well-documented risk analysis not only helps in managing potential threats but also demonstrates a thorough understanding of your business to potential investors, partners, and stakeholders.

11 Implementation Timeline

Creating an implementation timeline for a business plan is crucial for outlining the steps and deadlines required to achieve your business goals. Here is a step-by-step guide on how to write an implementation timeline.

Understand Your Business Plan
Understanding your business plan is crucial for successful execution and achieving your business goals.

Begin by thoroughly reading your business plan from start to finish. Pay attention to every section, including the executive summary, market analysis, business description, products or services, marketing strategy, operations plan, and financial projections.

Remember that your business plan will be different if your venture is a startup as opposed to a pre-existing business, and plan accordingly.

Clearly identify the primary objectives and goals outlined in your business plan. These are the overarching aims that your business seeks to achieve.

Clearly understand and articulate your unique value proposition. This is what sets your business apart from competitors. Why should customers choose you over other businesses in the same field? This is often outlined in the business description and marketing strategy sections.

Understand the target market and customer segments identified in your plan. Know who your customers are, their needs, and how your product or service fulfills those needs.

Review the marketing and sales strategies outlined in the plan. Understand how you plan to reach and acquire customers, as well as how you will promote and sell your products or services.

Analyze the competitive landscape presented in your business plan.

Understand who your competitors are, their strengths and weaknesses, and how your business will position itself in the market.

Delve into the operations plan to understand how your business will function on a day-to-day basis. This includes production processes, supply chain management, and any other operational considerations.

Examine the financial projections carefully. Understand the revenue forecasts, expense estimates, and profit margins. Identify key financial metrics such as break-even point and return on investment.

Identify and understand the assumptions made in the business plan. Recognize potential risks and challenges that could impact the successful implementation of the plan. Are your assumptions realistic? That is, are the assumptions being made in your business plan based on observable, verifiable data?

Connect the specific strategies outlined in your plan to the overall objectives. Understand how each strategy contributes to the achievement of your business goals. Always link all of the strategies in your business plan to your overall organization's objectives.

If your business plan includes information on the organizational structure, roles, and responsibilities, make sure you understand how each team member contributes to the overall success of the business. Eliminate redundant positions and develop hiring strategies for areas where your business lacks talent to fill key positions.

If there are parts of the business plan that are unclear, seek feedback from mentors, advisors, or team members. Clarify any ambiguities to ensure a shared understanding among stakeholders, investors, and lenders.

Remember that a business plan is a dynamic document. Regularly revisit and update it to reflect changes in the business environment, market conditions, and the internal dynamics of your company.

By thoroughly understanding your business plan, you'll be better equipped to make informed decisions, communicate effectively with stakeholders, and implement strategies that lead to the success of your business.

Identify Key Milestones

Milestones are significant achievements or events that mark progress toward your business goals.

Start by revisiting the goals and objectives outlined in your business plan. What are you trying to achieve in the short, medium, and long term? These objectives will help guide the identification of key milestones.

Break down your business plan into specific tasks and activities. This can be done by reviewing each section of the plan, such as marketing, operations, finance, and human resources, and identifying the actionable steps required.

Next, prioritize the activities based on their importance and impact on achieving your business goals. Some tasks may be prerequisites for others, so consider dependencies when prioritizing.

Engage with your team members or key stakeholders to gather input on critical activities and potential milestones. Different perspectives can help identify aspects that may have been overlooked.

Take into account external factors that may influence your business plan. This could include market conditions, regulatory changes, or technological advancements. Identify milestones that align with these external factors.

Assign estimated timeframes for each task or activity. Be realistic about the time required for completion. Consider the overall timeline for implementing the entire business plan.

Identify critical paths that are the sequences of tasks that must be completed on time for the overall plan to stay on schedule. Key milestones often lie along these critical paths.

Consider dividing your implementation plan into phases. Each phase may have its own set of milestones. This approach can make the implementation more manageable and allows for better monitoring of progress.

Define milestones in a way that is measurable. Stakeholders, investors, and lenders will be looking for quantifiable data. Instead of vague goals, use specific, quantifiable targets. This could include reaching a certain revenue level, acquiring a specific number of customers, or completing a project phase.

Identify both internal milestones (within your organization) and external milestones (involving external partners, customers, or market conditions). This comprehensive view ensures that all aspects of your business plan are considered. This is another aspect that stakeholders, investors and lenders will be looking for.

Confirm that each milestone aligns with the overall strategic objectives of your business. The achievement of each milestone should bring you closer to realizing your long-term vision.

Establish review points at regular intervals to assess progress. These reviews can help you identify whether adjustments are needed and whether the milestones are being achieved on schedule. Try to set these quarterly at a bare minimum. Monthly is often better, depending on the measures being evaluated.

Gather feedback from key stakeholders, including team members and advisors, to ensure that the identified milestones are realistic and achievable. Adjust as necessary based on the feedback received. Be sure to include all of your staff in soliciting feedback, and foster an atmosphere where such feedback is welcome.

Document the identified milestones in a clear and accessible format, such as a Gantt chart or project management software. Communicate the milestones to the relevant stakeholders to ensure everyone is on the same page.

Use a Gantt chart to visually represent the timeline. You can use tools like Microsoft Excel, Google Sheets, or specialized project management software.

A Gantt chart is a visual representation of a project schedule that displays the start and finish dates of various elements of a project. It provides a graphical illustration of a project's timeline, showing the sequence of tasks, their durations, and dependencies. Gantt charts are widely used in project management to help teams, stakeholders, and decision-makers understand the progress and schedule of a project.

Key components of a Gantt chart include:

Task Bars: Horizontal bars represent individual tasks or activities.

Timeline: A horizontal axis represents the project timeline, typically divided into days, weeks, or months.

Task Duration: The length of each task bar corresponds to the time required to complete the associated task.

Dependencies: Arrows or lines indicate dependencies between tasks, illustrating which tasks must be completed before others can begin.

Here's why a Gantt chart is important to a business plan: A Gantt chart provides a clear visual representation of the tasks and activities outlined in a business plan. This visual format helps stakeholders easily understand the sequence and timing of each task.

It also allows for effective timeline management by showing start and end dates for each task. This helps in coordinating and scheduling activities to ensure they are completed on time.

Gantt charts help identify task dependencies. Understanding which tasks are dependent on others is crucial for planning and avoiding delays.

The chart also aids in resource allocation by showing when specific resources, whether they are personnel, equipment, or finances, are needed during the project.

Gantt charts serve as a powerful communication tool. They help in communicating the project schedule to team members, stakeholders, and other involved parties.

As the project progresses, a Gantt chart can be updated to reflect the actual completion dates of tasks. This allows for easy tracking of project milestones and adjustments to the schedule as needed.

By visually representing the project schedule, Gantt charts facilitate the identification of potential risks and bottlenecks. This enables proactive risk management and the development of contingency plans.

Gantt charts provide decision-makers with a comprehensive overview of the project's status and progress. This visual representation aids in making informed decisions about resource allocation, timeline adjustments, and overall project strategy.

Gantt charts help align stakeholders on project timelines and expectations. When all parties involved can see the project schedule in a clear format, it promotes understanding and collaboration.

The visual nature of Gantt charts enhances overall project productivity. Team members can easily grasp the sequence of tasks and deadlines, reducing confusion and improving efficiency.

In the context of a business plan, using a Gantt chart is particularly valuable when outlining the implementation timeline. It provides a practical and accessible way to communicate how different aspects of the plan will be executed over time, fostering a shared understanding among team members and stakeholders.

The final step in identifying milestones is to break down each milestone into specific tasks and activities. Once identified, assign responsibilities for each task to individuals or teams within your organization. Hold regular meetings to solicit feedback from each member of the implementation team to assure that these milestones are being met on schedule and within budget.

Recognize and celebrate the achievement of key milestones. This not only boosts morale but also serves as motivation for the team to continue working toward the next set of goals.

Remember that the identification of milestones is an iterative process. As circumstances change or new information becomes available, be prepared to revisit and adjust your milestones accordingly. Regularly monitoring and updating your milestones will help keep your business plan dynamic and aligned with your evolving business needs.

Set Realistic Timeframes

Be realistic about the time required for each task in your implementation strategy. Consider factors such as resources, dependencies, and potential obstacles. Buffer in some extra time for unforeseen delays or adjustments. A good rule of thumb is to estimate how much time will be needed to achieve each milestone, then add about 20%.

Setting realistic timeframes for implementing a business strategy in a business plan is crucial for successful execution. Unrealistic timelines can lead to frustration, resource mismanagement, and failure to achieve desired outcomes.

Identify the key components and actions required to implement the strategy successfully. These should include the milestones established in the previous step.

Next, engage with key stakeholders, including team members, department heads, and relevant experts. Gather input on the time required for each task and factor in different perspectives.

Take into account external factors that may impact the implementation timeline. Consider market conditions, regulatory requirements, supplier lead times, and other external influences that could affect your strategy.

If applicable, draw on past experiences with similar projects or strategies. If yours is a previously existing business, you should already have this data and information. If a new business, you'll have to estimate based on what businesses similar to yours have experienced in the past. Identify any challenges or delays encountered in the past and use that knowledge to set more realistic timeframes for the current strategy.

Research industry standards and benchmarks for similar strategies. This can provide insights into typical timeframes for implementing comparable business strategies.

Determine the critical pathways or sequences of tasks that must be completed for the strategy to progress. Identify tasks that are prerequisites for others and prioritize them accordingly.

Consider dependencies between tasks. Tasks that are dependent on others should be scheduled in a way that accounts for the time needed to complete the predecessor tasks.

For each task, set three time estimates: *aggressive*, *realistic*, and *pessimistic*. This approach, known as PERT (Program Evaluation and Review Technique), helps in assessing the best and worst-case scenarios, allowing for a more balanced and realistic estimate.

Include the aforementioned buffer time or contingency periods in your overall timeline. This accounts for unexpected delays, changes in scope, or unforeseen challenges that may arise during the implementation process.

Evaluate the availability of resources, including personnel, technology, and financial resources. If specific resources are critical for certain tasks, ensure that their availability aligns with the proposed timeline.

Collaborate with your team to set realistic timeframes. Team members who are directly involved in the implementation process can provide valuable insights into the time required for their respective tasks.

Leverage project management tools and techniques to help with timeline estimation. Gantt charts, project scheduling software, and other tools can provide a visual representation of tasks and timelines, making it easier to identify potential bottlenecks.

Regularly review and adjust the timeline as needed. As the implementation progresses, new information may emerge, and adjustments may be necessary. Be flexible and willing to adapt to changing circumstances.

Clearly communicate the realistic timeframe to all stakeholders, including team members, investors, and partners. Managing expectations is essential for maintaining transparency and trust.

Implement a monitoring system to measure progress against the set timeframes. Regularly assess whether tasks are being completed on schedule, and if not, identify the reasons for any delays.

By following these steps, you can create a more accurate and realistic timeline for implementing your business strategy. This approach increases the likelihood of successful execution and helps your team stay focused and motivated throughout the implementation process.

Prioritize Tasks

Prioritizing tasks when implementing a business strategy is essential to ensure that resources are allocated efficiently, and the most critical activities are addressed first.

Start by thoroughly understanding the overall business strategy outlined in your business plan. Identify the key objectives and goals that the strategy aims to achieve.

Divide the business strategy into specific components or tasks. This could include marketing activities, product development, operational changes, financial adjustments, and more.

Identify tasks that are critical to the success of the overall strategy. These are tasks that, if delayed or not executed correctly, could significantly impact the achievement of strategic objectives.

Take into account task dependencies. Some tasks may need to be completed before others can start. Prioritize tasks that are prerequisites for subsequent activities.

Evaluate the resource requirements for each task, including personnel, finances, technology, and other necessary resources. Prioritize tasks that require scarce or specialized resources.

Consider the urgency of tasks. Some activities may have specific deadlines or time-sensitive elements. Prioritize tasks that must be completed within a certain timeframe.

Ensure that the prioritized tasks align directly with the strategic goals and objectives outlined in your business plan. This alignment ensures that resources are focused on activities that contribute most to your overarching strategy.

Consider the impact of tasks on various stakeholders, including customers, employees, investors, and partners. Prioritize tasks that have a significant positive impact on key stakeholders.

Employ a prioritization framework, such as the Eisenhower Matrix or MoSCoW method, to categorize tasks based on urgency and importance. This can help you visually prioritize tasks and allocate resources accordingly. A brief explanation of each is described below.

Eisenhower Matrix

The Eisenhower Matrix, also known as the Urgent-Important Matrix, is a time management and prioritization tool that helps individuals and teams categorize tasks based on their urgency and importance. The matrix was popularized by President Dwight D. Eisenhower and is often used to make informed decisions about task prioritization.

The matrix consists of four quadrants as pictured in the table below.

Quadrant I Urgent and Important	**Quadrant II** Important but Not Urgent
Tasks in this quadrant are both urgent and important. They require immediate attention and should be handled promptly. These tasks often relate to critical issues, emergencies, or deadlines.	Tasks in this quadrant are important but not urgent. These tasks contribute to long-term goals and strategic objectives. They should be planned and executed in a way that avoids unnecessary urgency. Proactive planning and prevention are key in this quadrant.
Quadrant III Urgent but Not Important	**Quadrant IV** Not Urgent and Not Important
Tasks in this quadrant are urgent but not important in the grand scheme of things. They may be distractions or activities that can be delegated to others. While they may require immediate attention, they don't contribute significantly to long-term goals.	Tasks in this quadrant are neither urgent nor important. They are low-priority activities that can be postponed, delegated, or eliminated. Spending too much time on tasks in this quadrant can lead to inefficiency and detract from more meaningful activities.

The Eisenhower Matrix helps individuals and teams prioritize tasks by placing them in the appropriate quadrant. The goal is to focus on Quadrant II tasks, as they contribute the most to long-term success and can prevent issues from becoming urgent.

This approach encourages a strategic and proactive mindset, rather than being solely reactive to immediate demands.

In a business implementation plan, the Eisenhower Matrix can be a valuable tool for prioritizing tasks associated with the execution of the plan. It helps ensure that efforts are directed toward activities that align with the overall strategy and contribute to the business's long-term success.

MoSCoW Method

The MoSCoW method is a prioritization technique commonly used in project management to categorize and prioritize tasks based on their importance and urgency. The method helps teams focus on the most critical aspects of a project, ensuring that essential requirements and objectives are addressed first.

The acronym "MoSCoW" stands for:

M - *Must have*: Critical requirements or tasks that are essential for the project's success. These items are non-negotiable and must be included in the implementation of the business strategy.

S - *Should have*: Important requirements or tasks that are significant but may be negotiable. These items contribute to the project's success but are not as critical as "Must haves."

C - *Could have*: Desirable requirements or tasks that would be nice to have but are not crucial. These items can be considered if time and resources permit but are not a priority.

W – *Won't have (at this time)*: Tasks that are explicitly excluded from the current scope. These items are deferred to a later phase or are intentionally left out of the implementation plan.

Here's how to use the MoSCoW method when implementing a business strategy:

1. Begin by identifying and listing all the requirements or tasks associated with the implementation of your business strategy. These could include activities from various aspects of the business, such as marketing, operations, finance, and technology.
2. Categorize each requirement or task into one of the MoSCoW categories: *Must have, Should have, Could have,* or *Won't have.*

3. Within each category, prioritize items based on their relative importance. This step helps provide a more nuanced understanding of priorities within each broad category.
4. Discuss the prioritized list with key stakeholders, including team members, department heads, and any other relevant parties. Gain consensus on the priorities and ensure that all stakeholders have a shared understanding of the significance of each item.
5. Regularly review and refine the MoSCoW list as the business landscape evolves or as new information becomes available. Adjust priorities based on changing circumstances and feedback from stakeholders.
6. Once priorities are established, create detailed implementation plans for the "Must have" and "Should have" items. These plans should outline specific tasks, timelines, and responsible parties for each priority.
7. Allocate resources, including personnel, budget, and technology, based on the priorities set by the MoSCoW method. Ensure that the most critical tasks receive the necessary resources for successful implementation.
8. Implement a monitoring and tracking system to assess progress on the prioritized tasks. Regularly review whether the implementation is aligning with the established priorities and make adjustments as needed.
9. Clearly communicate the MoSCoW priorities to all relevant stakeholders. Transparency about priorities helps maintain focus and ensures that efforts are directed toward the most critical aspects of the business strategy.
10. As the implementation progresses, iterate on the MoSCoW list and update priorities based on real-time feedback, changes in the business environment, or emerging opportunities or challenges.

By applying the MoSCoW method, your implementation strategy can systematically prioritize your efforts and resources during the implementation of your business strategy, leading to more focused and effective execution.

Consider Risk and Uncertainty

Evaluate the level of risk associated with each task or milestone in your implementation plan. High-risk tasks that could have a substantial impact on the project's success may need to be addressed early in the implementation process.

Strike a balance between short-term and long-term goals. While it is important to address immediate priorities, ensure that you're also laying the groundwork for long-term success.

Involve key stakeholders, including team members and department heads, in the prioritization process. Their input can provide valuable insights and ensure a more comprehensive perspective.

Regularly reassess and adjust task priorities as the business landscape evolves. Changes in market conditions, customer preferences, or internal factors may necessitate adjustments to the task prioritization.

Clearly communicate task priorities to the entire team. Ensure that everyone understands the rationale behind the prioritization and the collective focus on strategic goals.

Implement a monitoring system to track progress on prioritized tasks. Regularly review and assess whether tasks are being completed according to the established priorities. This will help to prevent risk before it occurs, and to minimize it should unforeseen risks appear.

By following these steps, you can develop a strategic approach to task prioritization that aligns with your business plan and helps to avoid risk. This ensures that your team focuses on the most critical activities, increasing the likelihood of successful strategy implementation.

Include Key Functional Areas

Ensure that your timeline covers key functional areas of your business, such as marketing, operations, finance, and human resources.

Regularly monitor progress in these key functional areas against the overall implementation timeline.

Conduct regular reviews with your team to address any challenges and make necessary adjustments to the timeline to insure that the key functional areas are being addressed in a timely manner.

Keep stakeholders, including team members, investors, and partners, informed about the progress. This is especially important where key functional areas are concerned.

Communicate any changes to the timeline promptly.

Anticipate potential risks and challenges. Develop contingency plans for addressing issues that may arise in key functional areas during implementation.

Identify alternative approaches or solutions for potential roadblocks.

Once you have refined and validated the implementation timeline, finalize the document. Distribute the timeline to all relevant stakeholders and ensure everyone is aware of their roles and responsibilities.

Regularly review and update the implementation timeline as needed. Adjust timelines based on the changing needs of the business, market conditions, or other relevant factors.

Remember, flexibility is key when creating an implementation timeline. Circumstances may change, and the timeline may need to be adjusted accordingly. Regularly revisit and update the timeline to ensure that your business plan stays on track.

12 Monitoring and Evaluation

The Monitoring and Evaluation (M&E) section of a business plan is crucial for assessing the progress, effectiveness, and impact of your business activities. It involves systematically tracking and evaluating the implementation of your business plan to ensure that goals are being met and to identify areas for improvement.

In this chapter we'll discuss how to write the Monitoring and Evaluation section of your business plan.

Start by providing a brief overview of the importance of monitoring and evaluation in the context of your business plan. Explain the purpose of the M&E section and how it aligns with the overall goals of your business. Some important components to cover are outlined below.

Objectives

Outlining objectives in a business plan helps provide clarity on what your business aims to achieve. Objectives should be Specific, Measurable, Achievable, Relevant, and Time-bound (SMART).

Begin by summarizing your key business objectives. Concisely highlight the main goals your business aims to achieve.

Next, align your objectives with the broader mission and vision statements of your business.

Clarify how achieving these objectives contributes to the overall mission and vision.

Categorize your objectives to make them more manageable and understandable. Common categories include financial, operational, marketing, and social responsibility objectives.

Specify financial goals such as revenue targets, profit margins, return on investment (ROI), and other financial metrics.

Include short-term and long-term financial objectives.

Outline objectives related to the day-to-day operations of the business. This may include production efficiency, supply chain optimization, quality improvement, and other operational efficiencies.

Define marketing and sales goals to drive business growth. Include objectives related to market share, customer acquisition, customer retention, and branding.

Specify objectives related to the development, improvement, or expansion of your products or services. This may include launching new products, improving existing ones, or entering new markets.

Clearly state objectives related to customer satisfaction, relationship building, and stakeholder engagement. Consider objectives that reflect your commitment to customer service and stakeholder value.

Include objectives related to hiring, training, and retaining employees.

Address organizational development goals, such as improving workplace culture and leadership development.

If applicable, outline objectives related to corporate social responsibility (CSR) and sustainability. This could involve initiatives to reduce environmental impact, support community development, or promote ethical business practices.

Ensure each objective is SMART: Specific, Measurable, Achievable, Relevant, and Time-bound. Clearly define success criteria and how progress will be measured.

Identify any dependencies or relationships between different objectives. Consider how achieving one objective may impact or contribute to the achievement of others.

Describe how progress toward objectives will be monitored and evaluated. Specify the frequency of assessments and the metrics that will be used to measure success. At a minimum, quarterly is a good place to start, although some metrics will need to be monthly or even weekly.

Acknowledge potential risks and challenges that may affect the achievement of objectives. Outline strategies to mitigate these risks in the appropriate section(s) of your business plan.

Ensure that your objectives align with the overall business plan and are consistent with your business's mission, vision, and values.

Highlight how achieving these objectives benefits various stakeholders, including customers, employees, investors, and the community.

By following these steps, you can create a well-structured outline of objectives that not only guides your business plan but also serves as a roadmap for achieving success in your business endeavors.

Key Performance Indicators (KPIs)

Describing Key Performance Indicators (KPIs) in the Monitoring and

Evaluation (M&E) section of a business plan is essential for measuring progress, tracking performance, and ensuring that your business is on track to achieve its objectives.

Provide a brief introduction to KPIs, explaining their role in measuring and assessing the performance of your business plan. Emphasize that KPIs are specific metrics aligned with critical business objectives.

Clearly state how each KPI aligns with specific objectives outlined in the business plan. Demonstrate the direct correlation between the chosen KPIs and the success criteria of your business.

Define each KPI and explain how it will be measured. Specify the unit of measurement and the methodology for collecting and analyzing the data associated with each KPI.

Establish baseline values for each KPI, representing the starting point or current performance level. Set realistic and achievable target values for each KPI, indicating the desired level of performance at specific points in time.

Outline how often each KPI will be measured and monitored. Specify the frequency of data collection and reporting, whether it's daily, weekly, monthly, quarterly, or annually.

Clearly define who within the organization is responsible for tracking and reporting each KPI. Assign accountability to specific individuals or teams to ensure that the monitoring process is well-managed.

Identify the sources of data for each KPI. Specify whether data will be collected from internal sources, external sources, surveys, financial reports, or other relevant channels.

Describe the methods used to collect data for each KPI. Highlight any tools, surveys, or systems employed to gather accurate and reliable information.

Establish acceptable thresholds or tolerance levels for each KPI. Define the range within which performance is considered acceptable, and indicate when intervention or corrective action is required.

Explain how the data collected for each KPI will be interpreted and analyzed. Discuss the significance of trends, variations, or deviations from the expected values.

Outline how KPI results will be communicated within the organization. Specify the format of reports and the key stakeholders who will receive information on KPI performance.

Emphasize how insights from KPIs will be used to drive continuous improvement. Discuss how the organization will adapt strategies based on KPI data to enhance overall business performance.

Mention any technology or tools that will be used for KPI monitoring and reporting. Discuss how these tools enhance efficiency and accuracy in tracking and analyzing KPI data.

Consider comparing current KPI values with historical data to provide context and insights into trends over time. Evaluate the impact of past actions on current performance.

Address potential risks associated with monitoring and measuring KPIs. Describe strategies and contingency plans for mitigating these risks and ensuring the reliability of KPI data.

By incorporating these elements into the description of KPIs in the Monitoring and Evaluation section, you provide a comprehensive framework for effectively tracking, analyzing, and leveraging key performance indicators to drive the success of your business plan.

Data Collection Methods

In the Monitoring and Evaluation (M&E) section of a business plan, describing the data collection methods is crucial for gathering accurate and relevant information to assess the progress and impact of your business activities.

Start by emphasizing the importance of data collection in evaluating the success of your business plan. Briefly explain that data collection methods will be used to gather information on key performance indicators (KPIs) and other relevant metrics.

Clearly outline the specific methods chosen for data collection. Discuss why these methods are appropriate for the objectives and KPIs identified in the business plan.

If applicable, distinguish between quantitative and qualitative data collection methods. Quantitative methods involve numerical data and can include surveys, financial reports, and website analytics. Qualitative methods involve non-numerical data and can include interviews, focus groups, and case studies.

If surveys or questionnaires are part of your data collection strategy, describe the survey design, target audience, and distribution method. Mention any tools or platforms used to create and distribute surveys, and explain how the collected data will be analyzed.

If interviews are part of your data collection plan, specify who will be interviewed (e.g., stakeholders, customers, employees) and the interview format (structured, semi-structured, or unstructured). Discuss how interview data will be recorded, transcribed, and analyzed.

Explain how observational methods will be used, if applicable. Clarify what will be observed, who will conduct the observations, and how the observational data will be recorded and analyzed.

Identify any existing data sources that will be utilized, such as financial reports, sales data, or customer feedback. Discuss how this existing data will be integrated into the overall data collection process.

If your business relies on digital platforms, describe any data logging or tracking tools in use. Discuss how these tools will capture and record relevant data automatically.

If applicable, explain the sampling techniques used in quantitative data collection. Specify the sampling size, method, and how it represents the larger population.

Mention if you plan to use triangulation, which involves using multiple methods to validate or corroborate findings. Explain how this approach enhances the reliability and validity of your data.

Discuss measures taken to ensure data security and privacy. Address how sensitive information will be handled, stored, and protected.

If necessary, outline any training provided to individuals involved in data collection. Discuss how capacity building contributes to the accuracy and consistency of data collection.

Provide a timeline indicating when data collection activities will take place. Align the timeline with the overall business plan schedule and milestones.

Discuss measures in place for quality assurance during data collection. Include protocols for data validation, reliability checks, and addressing potential biases.

Emphasize that the data collection methods will be continuously monitored and adapted as needed. Discuss how feedback loops will inform adjustments to ensure the ongoing relevance and effectiveness of the data collection process.

If applicable, outline the budget and resources allocated to support data collection efforts. Discuss any technology or tools that require financial investment.

By thoroughly explaining your data collection methods in the Monitoring and Evaluation section, you demonstrate a systematic and thoughtful approach to gathering the information needed to assess the performance of your business plan.

Data Analysis and Reporting

The Data Analysis and Reporting section translates raw data into actionable insights. It involves systematically examining collected data to assess performance, measure progress against objectives, and inform decision-making.

Begin by emphasizing the importance of data analysis and reporting in the M&E process. Explain that these activities are essential for extracting meaningful insights and informing strategic decision-making.

Detail how quantitative data will be analyzed, including statistical methods, if applicable. Describe how financial reports, sales data, and other numerical information will be processed and interpreted.

Outline methods for analyzing qualitative data, such as thematic analysis, content analysis, or narrative interpretation. Explain how insights from interviews, focus groups, and open-ended survey responses will be extracted.

Discuss procedures for validating and cleaning the data before analysis. Address any outliers, inconsistencies, or errors that may impact the accuracy of the results.

Explain the process of cross-referencing data from multiple sources for triangulation. Describe how this method enhances the reliability and validity of the analysis.

Highlight how Key Performance Indicators (KPIs) will be tracked and monitored over time. Illustrate trends, patterns, and variations in KPIs to provide a comprehensive understanding of performance.

Conduct comparative analysis against baseline values and target benchmarks. Assess whether the business is on track to meet its objectives and identify areas that require attention.

Discuss how data will be visualized for easier interpretation. Consider using charts, graphs, dashboards, and other visual aids to communicate complex information effectively.

Specify the frequency at which data analysis will occur. Align the analysis schedule with the frequency of data collection and reporting.

Outline the format and structure of the reports that will be generated. Include sections for key findings, trends, challenges, and recommendations.

Discuss whether there will be specific reports tailored for different stakeholders. Customize reports to address the interests and concerns of various audiences, such as investors, employees, or regulatory bodies.

Provide a narrative that contextualizes the data and findings. Explain the significance of the results in relation to the business's overall goals and objectives.

 Interpret the findings in a way that is clear and accessible. Avoid jargon and technical language that may be challenging for non-experts to understand.

Emphasize how the analysis generates actionable insights. Discuss how these insights will inform decision-making and will drive strategic adjustments.

Offer recommendations for continuous improvement based on the analysis. Propose strategies and actions to address challenges and enhance performance.

Integrate feedback loops into the reporting process. Demonstrate how insights from reports will inform adjustments in the business plan and strategies.

Specify the timeline for generating and disseminating reports. Align reporting timelines with business plan milestones and review cycles.

Ensure that reports are easily accessible to relevant stakeholders. Emphasize transparency in presenting both successes and challenges.

Discuss the budget and resources allocated for data analysis and reporting. Address any technology or analytical tools that require financial investment.

Outline plans for reviewing and auditing the data analysis process. Ensure that the analysis methods and results are subject to periodic reviews for quality assurance.

By thoroughly explaining the data analysis and reporting process in the M&E section of your business plan, you demonstrate a commitment to evidence-based decision-making and continuous improvement, crucial elements for achieving long-term success.

Risk Assessment and Mitigation

This section helps identify potential challenges and outlines strategies to minimize or overcome them.

Begin by emphasizing the importance of identifying and addressing potential risks in the business plan. Explain that risk assessment is a proactive approach to anticipate challenges that may impact the achievement of business objectives.

Enumerate and describe various types of risks that could affect your business. Categorize risks into different groups such as operational, financial, market-related, legal, and strategic risks.

Assess the likelihood of each identified risk occurring. Evaluate the potential impact or severity of each risk on the business.

Prioritize risks based on their likelihood and impact. Focus on addressing high-priority risks that have the potential to significantly affect business objectives.

Identify risks related to day-to-day operations, such as supply chain disruptions, technology failures, or employee turnover. Develop strategies to mitigate the impact of these risks on business continuity.

Address financial risks such as market fluctuations, economic downturns, or unexpected expenses. Outline financial contingency plans, reserve funds, or strategies to diversify revenue streams.

Evaluate risks related to market dynamics, competition, and changes in consumer behavior. Develop marketing and market research strategies to adapt to changing market conditions.

Identify potential legal and regulatory risks that may arise. Ensure compliance with laws and regulations, and establish a legal support system to address potential issues.

Assess risks related to the execution of the business plan and achievement of strategic objectives. Develop alternative strategies and contingency plans to pivot if necessary.

If applicable, address risks related to cybersecurity threats. Implement security measures to protect sensitive data and ensure the integrity of digital operations.

Evaluate risks associated with damage to the company's reputation. Develop a crisis communication plan to address potential reputational challenges.

For each identified risk, propose specific mitigation strategies. Clearly outline the actions that will be taken to reduce the likelihood or impact of each risk.

Establish monitoring mechanisms and early warning systems for potential risks. Regularly assess the risk landscape and update mitigation strategies as needed.

Develop contingency plans that outline specific actions to be taken if a risk materializes. Include response plans that define roles and responsibilities in the event of a crisis.

Consider conducting scenario planning exercises to simulate the impact of various risks. Use scenario planning to refine and enhance mitigation strategies.

Integrate risk assessment into the overall monitoring and evaluation process. Discuss how the organization will learn from risks and continuously improve its risk management strategies.

Emphasize the importance of transparent communication regarding risks. Address how stakeholders will be informed of potential risks and the steps taken to mitigate them.

Allocate budget and resources for risk mitigation strategies. Ensure that financial provisions are made for addressing potential risks.

Stress the iterative nature of risk assessment and mitigation. Demonstrate a commitment to learning from experiences and refining risk management strategies over time.

By comprehensively explaining risk assessment and mitigation strategies in the Evaluation and Monitoring section, you instill confidence in stakeholders and show that your business plan is well-prepared to navigate uncertainties and challenges.

Feedback and Learning

This section focuses on mechanisms for collecting feedback, analyzing it, and leveraging insights to enhance business performance.

Begin by emphasizing the significance of feedback and learning in the context of monitoring and evaluation. Highlight that these components are instrumental in adapting strategies and optimizing business performance.

Identify the various channels through which feedback will be collected. Include mechanisms such as customer surveys, employee feedback sessions, stakeholder consultations, and other relevant platforms.

Emphasize the importance of engaging with key stakeholders for valuable perspectives. Discuss how feedback from customers, employees, investors, and other stakeholders will be actively sought.

Highlight strategies for collecting feedback from employees. Discuss regular feedback sessions, surveys, and mechanisms to ensure an open communication culture within the organization.

Explain how customer feedback will be collected and analyzed. Discuss methods such as surveys, online reviews, and customer service interactions.

If applicable, address feedback mechanisms involving vendors and business partners. Discuss regular communication channels and feedback loops with external collaborators.

Detail the design and deployment of surveys and questionnaires. Specify the frequency, target audience, and key topics covered in these instruments.

Discuss plans for conducting focus group discussions. Explain how insights gathered from focus groups will contribute to the learning process.

Address how customer complaints and issues will be handled. Outline a structured process for receiving, tracking, and resolving complaints.

Explain the methods for analyzing feedback data. Discuss how quantitative data will be processed and how qualitative insights will be extracted and categorized.

Acknowledge and highlight instances of success. Discuss how positive outcomes will be analyzed to identify factors contributing to success.

Discuss how challenges and setbacks will be analyzed. Emphasize a problem-solving approach and the lessons that can be learned from overcoming difficulties.

Address how knowledge gained from feedback and learning will be shared within the organization. Discuss methods for disseminating insights to relevant teams and individuals.

Highlight that the primary purpose of feedback and learning is to inform strategic adjustments. Discuss how insights gained will influence decision-making and the evolution of business strategies.

Emphasize that feedback and learning are part of an ongoing, iterative process. Illustrate how the organization is committed to a continuous improvement cycle.

If necessary, discuss plans for training and capacity building based on feedback. Explain how the organization will invest in skill development and knowledge enhancement.

Integrate feedback and learning insights with key performance metrics. Demonstrate how these insights contribute to the refinement of performance indicators.

Discuss how changes resulting from feedback and learning will be communicated. Ensure transparency in communicating adjustments to stakeholders.

Allocate resources for feedback mechanisms, analysis tools, and the implementation of improvements. Ensure that budget provisions support the organization's commitment to learning.

By incorporating these elements into the Feedback and Learning section of your business plan, you emphasize the importance of being responsive to stakeholder input, learning from experiences, and continuously improving business strategies and operations.

Timeline and Milestones

Including a timeline and milestones is essential for setting clear expectations, tracking progress, and ensuring that the business stays on course to achieve its objectives.

Begin by introducing the concept of a timeline and milestones within the context of monitoring and evaluation. Explain that this section provides a structured framework for tracking progress over time.

Define a comprehensive timeline that covers the entire duration of the business plan. Break down the timeline into manageable intervals, such as months, quarters, or years, depending on the nature of your business and objectives.

Clearly define the key milestones that mark significant achievements or stages of the business plan. Milestones should align with the broader objectives and goals outlined in the business plan.

Include both quantifiable and qualitative milestones. Quantifiable milestones are measurable and can include targets like revenue goals, customer acquisition numbers, or product development milestones. Qualitative milestones may include achievements in brand recognition, customer satisfaction, or market positioning.

Align specific milestones with each major objective outlined in the business plan. For example, if your objective is to launch a new product, milestones could include completing product development, conducting market research, and executing a marketing campaign.

Identify dependencies and establish the sequencing of milestones. Clarify if the achievement of one milestone is dependent on the completion of another and how these interdependencies will be managed.

Assign responsibility for each milestone to specific individuals or teams. Clearly define who is accountable for the successful achievement of each milestone.

Specify the frequency at which progress towards milestones will be monitored. Indicate whether monitoring will be continuous, weekly, monthly, or based on other relevant intervals.

Associate performance metrics and indicators with each milestone. Define the key performance indicators (KPIs) that will be used to measure progress.

Establish baseline values for relevant metrics. Set realistic and achievable target values for each milestone to provide a basis for comparison.

Acknowledge that timelines and milestones may need to be adjusted based on real-time feedback and changing circumstances. Discuss the mechanisms in place for adapting the timeline if needed.

Discuss how achievements of milestones will be communicated within the organization. Consider if and how these achievements will be shared with external stakeholders.

Allocate budgetary resources to support the achievement of milestones. Ensure that necessary resources are available at each stage of the timeline.

Address potential risks that may lead to delays in achieving milestones. Outline strategies and contingency plans to mitigate these risks and prevent significant disruptions.

Emphasize the importance of celebrating and recognizing milestone achievements. Consider how positive reinforcement can contribute to team motivation and morale.

Integrate the timeline and milestones with the broader monitoring and evaluation process. Discuss how insights gained from progress tracking will inform adjustments and improvements.

Specify review points and evaluation periods throughout the timeline. Discuss how the organization will formally assess progress, make informed decisions, and potentially recalibrate strategies.

Emphasize transparency in reporting progress towards milestones. Discuss how reports will be shared with stakeholders and made accessible within the organization.

Emphasize that the timeline and milestones are part of an iterative process. Discuss how the organization will learn from the achievement or deviation from milestones and apply those learnings to future planning.

By incorporating these elements into the Timeline and Milestones section of your business plan, you provide a structured and strategic framework for monitoring progress, celebrating successes, and navigating potential challenges on the path to achieving your business objectives.

Budget and Resources

The budget and resources is necessary of overviewing financial and non-financial resources to assure they are allocated to effectively carry out monitoring and evaluation activities

Start by emphasizing the importance of allocating sufficient resources for monitoring and evaluation. Explain that the budget and resources section ensures the effective implementation of the monitoring and

Outline the specific resources required for monitoring and evaluation activities. Include both financial resources (budget) and non-financial resources, such as personnel, technology, and data collection tools.

Provide a detailed breakdown of the budget allocated for monitoring and evaluation. Specify the amounts allocated to different components, such as personnel costs, technology expenses, training, and any external consultancy services.

Detail the costs associated with personnel involved in monitoring and evaluation. Include salaries, benefits, and any additional costs related to training or capacity-building initiatives.

Specify the budget allocated for technology and tools used in data collection, analysis, and reporting. Include costs for software, hardware, data storage, and any specialized tools needed for effective monitoring and evaluation.

Allocate budgetary resources for training programs related to monitoring and evaluation. Include costs for workshops, courses, or certifications that enhance the skills of personnel involved in the process.

If applicable, detail any budget allocated for external consultants or services. Explain the specific expertise or services these external entities will provide in support of monitoring and evaluation.

If monitoring and evaluation activities involve fieldwork or travel, allocate a budget for travel and logistics. Include expenses for transportation, accommodation, and any other logistical requirements.

Specify the budget for data collection efforts. Include costs associated with surveys, interviews, focus groups, and any other methods used to collect data.

Allocate resources for the creation and dissemination of reports. Include costs for designing reports, printing or digital dissemination, and communication efforts related to sharing findings.

Allocate a budget for quality assurance measures. Include costs associated with data validation, audits, and any other processes aimed at ensuring the accuracy and reliability of the evaluation.

If applicable, allocate resources for technology infrastructure. Include costs for maintaining servers, databases, and other technological infrastructure essential for monitoring and evaluation activities.

Set aside a contingency fund within the budget to address unforeseen challenges or additional resource needs. This fund can act as a buffer in case of unexpected circumstances that may impact the monitoring and evaluation process.

Consider the frequency and duration of monitoring activities when allocating resources. Ensure that the budget covers the entire monitoring and evaluation timeline, including ongoing monitoring and periodic evaluations.

Emphasize how the allocated budget aligns with the overall business objectives. Justify resource allocation by linking it to the expected impact on achieving business goals.

Discuss the anticipated benefits derived from the allocated resources. Include a brief cost-benefit analysis to demonstrate the value of the resources invested in monitoring and evaluation.

Ensure alignment with the overall financial projections presented in the business plan. Provide a cohesive narrative that connects the budget for monitoring and evaluation with the broader financial strategy.

Discuss how the utilization of allocated resources will be monitored and reported. Establish reporting mechanisms that ensure accountability and transparency in resource utilization.

Emphasize that the budget and resource allocation process is iterative. Discuss how insights from monitoring and evaluation activities will inform adjustments to the budget for future cycles.

By thoroughly explaining the budget and resources in the Evaluation and Monitoring section, you demonstrate a commitment to dedicating the necessary resources to ensure effective monitoring and evaluation processes, ultimately contributing to the success and improvement of your business activities.

Responsibilities and Roles

In the Evaluation and Monitoring section, detailing responsibilities and roles is crucial for establishing accountability, ensuring clarity on who is responsible for what, and facilitating the effective implementation of monitoring and evaluation activities.

Start by introducing the concept of responsibilities and roles within the context of monitoring and evaluation. Explain that this section outlines the key individuals or teams responsible for various aspects of the monitoring and evaluation process.

Clearly define the individual or team that holds overall accountability for monitoring and evaluation. Specify their role in overseeing the entire process and ensuring that goals and objectives are met.

Identify the team responsible for day-to-day monitoring activities. Outline the specific tasks and responsibilities of this team, including data collection, tracking key performance indicators (KPIs), and ensuring the timely execution of monitoring activities.

Specify the team or individuals responsible for conducting evaluations. Define their roles in designing evaluation methodologies, analyzing data, and producing comprehensive evaluation reports.

If applicable, outline the roles of individuals or teams responsible for data collection. Specify the methods and tools they will use and emphasize the importance of accurate and timely data collection.

Assign responsibility for managing the technology and tools used in monitoring and evaluation. Specify who is in charge of maintaining databases, using analytical tools, and ensuring that technology infrastructure is functional.

Define the individuals or team responsible for quality assurance. Outline their roles in validating data, conducting audits, and ensuring that the monitoring and evaluation process adheres to quality standards.

Assign roles for engaging with stakeholders during the monitoring and evaluation process. Specify who will be responsible for gathering feedback, conducting interviews, and ensuring that stakeholder perspectives are considered.

Identify the team or individual responsible for reporting and communication. Outline their roles in preparing reports, disseminating findings, and maintaining transparent communication with internal and external stakeholders.

Ensure that roles are clearly defined for integrating monitoring and evaluation with other business functions. - Discuss how information and insights from monitoring and evaluation will be shared with relevant teams for strategic decision-making.

Assign responsibility for training and capacity-building initiatives. Specify who will be in charge of enhancing the skills and knowledge of individuals involved in monitoring and evaluation.

Designate responsibility for managing the timeline and milestones. Specify who will be accountable for ensuring that monitoring and evaluation activities align with the established timeline.

Identify the individual or team responsible for overseeing the budget allocated to monitoring and evaluation. Outline their roles in managing expenses, ensuring cost-effectiveness, and reporting on budget utilization.

If applicable, establish a team or designate individuals responsible for continuous improvement. Define their roles in analyzing feedback, learning from experiences, and implementing adjustments to enhance the monitoring and evaluation process.

Assign roles related to risk management within the monitoring and evaluation context. Specify who is responsible for identifying potential risks, implementing mitigation strategies, and addressing unforeseen challenges.

Emphasize the importance of cross-functional collaboration. Specify how teams responsible for monitoring and evaluation will collaborate with other departments or teams within the organization.

Assign roles for training and onboarding new team members involved in monitoring and evaluation. Specify how knowledge transfer and skill development will be managed.

Assign responsibility for documenting the monitoring and evaluation process. Emphasize roles in knowledge sharing to ensure that insights and best practices are shared within the organization.

Designate roles for regular reviews and reporting. Specify who is responsible for assessing the effectiveness of monitoring and evaluation activities and providing periodic reports to relevant stakeholders.

By detailing responsibilities and roles in the Evaluation and Monitoring section of your business plan, you provide a foundation for a structured and accountable approach to the monitoring and evaluation process, fostering transparency and collaboration among team members involved in these critical activities.

Continuous Improvement

Incorporating a continuous improvement framework in your business plan demonstrates a commitment to learning from experiences and refining strategies over time.

Begin by highlighting the significance of continuous improvement within the monitoring and evaluation process. Explain that this section outlines the mechanisms and strategies in place to learn from data, feedback, and experiences for ongoing refinement.

Emphasize the organization's commitment to learning from both successes and challenges identified through monitoring and evaluation activities. Clearly state that continuous improvement is an integral part of the organizational culture.

Discuss the establishment of feedback loops within the monitoring and evaluation process. Emphasize how feedback from various sources, including stakeholders, employees, and customers, will be actively sought and integrated.

Highlight the organization's commitment to data-driven decision-making. Discuss how insights gained from data analysis will inform strategic decisions and adjustments to business plans.

Clearly state that the organization is open to adjusting strategies based on the findings of monitoring and evaluation. Discuss how the business plan will be a living document that evolves with new insights.

Emphasize that the monitoring and evaluation process is designed to generate actionable insights. Discuss how these insights will be used to identify areas for improvement and inform decision-making.

Specify regular review points within the business plan timeline. Discuss how these reviews will provide opportunities to reflect on progress, identify lessons learned, and make necessary adjustments.

If applicable, discuss plans for post-implementation evaluation of major initiatives or projects. Explain how the organization will assess the outcomes and impacts of implemented strategies.

Consider incorporating scenario planning into the continuous improvement framework. Discuss how the organization will engage in strategic foresight to anticipate potential future challenges and opportunities.

Explicitly state that successes will be analyzed as part of the continuous improvement process. Discuss how positive outcomes will be studied to identify contributing factors and best practices.

Emphasize the organization's commitment to learning from challenges and setbacks. Discuss how the insights gained from addressing challenges will contribute to resilience and adaptability.

Discuss how continuous improvement efforts will be integrated with key performance metrics. Explain that insights from continuous improvement will influence the refinement of performance indicators.

If necessary, discuss plans for capacity building based on continuous improvement insights. Explain how the organization will invest in skill development and knowledge enhancement to support ongoing improvement.

Highlight the importance of fostering an innovative culture. Discuss how the organization will encourage experimentation and learning from pilot projects.

Emphasize the establishment of an organizational learning culture. Discuss how the organization encourages curiosity, exploration, and a mindset of continuous learning among its members.

Discuss mechanisms for soliciting feedback and involvement from employees in the continuous improvement process. Emphasize that employees are integral contributors to the organization's learning and growth.

Discuss how changes resulting from continuous improvement efforts will be communicated. Ensure transparency in communicating adjustments to stakeholders, employees, and other relevant parties.

Align continuous improvement efforts with feedback received from stakeholders. Discuss how stakeholder perspectives will be considered in refining strategies and operations.

Allocate resources within the budget specifically for continuous improvement initiatives. Emphasize that the organization is dedicating financial resources to support ongoing learning and refinement.

Outline plans for reviewing and auditing the continuous improvement process. Ensure that the process itself is subject to periodic evaluation for effectiveness and efficiency.

By incorporating these elements into the Continuous Improvement section of your business plan, you communicate a commitment to agility, adaptability, and a culture of learning, which are essential for long-term success in a dynamic business environment.

Appendix

The appendix of the Evaluation and Monitoring section is an opportunity to include supplementary materials that provide additional depth and support to the main content. While your particular organization might not have all of these, or might have different supporting documents, this list will give you a good idea of the types of documents that should be included in your appendices.

Detailed Data Sets

If there are extensive datasets related to your monitoring and evaluation, consider including a selection of key data points or the entire dataset in the appendix. This is especially relevant if stakeholders may want to delve deeper into the quantitative aspects of your analysis.

Survey Instruments

Include copies of the survey instruments or questionnaires used in data collection. This adds transparency and allows stakeholders to understand the specific questions asked.

Interview Protocols

If interviews or focus groups were part of your data collection process, include the protocols or guides used for these interactions. This helps stakeholders understand the context and structure of qualitative data collection.

Sampling Methods

Provide details on the methods used for sampling if applicable. Include information on how participants or data points were selected, and why certain sampling methods were chosen.

Detailed Budget Breakdown

If your monitoring and evaluation activities have a dedicated budget, include a detailed breakdown of the expenses. This adds transparency and helps stakeholders understand the allocation of resources.

Technology and Tools Documentation

If specific technologies or tools were used for data collection, analysis, or reporting, include documentation or user manuals in the appendix. This is particularly relevant if stakeholders may need to interact with these tools.

List of Key Performance Indicators (KPIs)

Provide a comprehensive list of the key performance indicators (KPIs) that were monitored. Include baseline values, target values, and actual results if available.

Graphs and Charts

Include any additional graphs, charts, or visual representations of data that were not included in the main body of the document. This can provide a more detailed visual understanding of trends.

Case Studies

If applicable, include case studies that illustrate specific instances or examples related to the monitoring and evaluation process. These can add context and depth to your overall narrative.

Documentation of Continuous Improvement Initiatives

If there are specific continuous improvement initiatives or adjustments made based on monitoring and evaluation findings, include documentation outlining these changes and their rationale.

Training Materials

If training and capacity-building were part of your monitoring and evaluation strategy, include training materials or outlines used to educate team members.

Timeline and Milestones Chart

Include a visual representation of the timeline and milestones, especially if it helps stakeholders understand the chronological sequence of monitoring and evaluation activities.

Risk Assessment Documentation

If you conducted a detailed risk assessment, include the documentation outlining identified risks, their likelihood, potential impact, and mitigation strategies.

Feedback and Survey Results

Include detailed results from surveys and feedback mechanisms. This could include both quantitative results and qualitative insights.

Certificates of Training or Qualifications

If training programs or capacity-building initiatives were conducted, include certificates or documentation related to the qualifications of team members involved in monitoring and evaluation.

Legal and Ethical Documentation

Include any legal or ethical documentation related to data collection, privacy, and compliance with relevant regulations.

External Consultant Reports

If external consultants were involved, include their reports or findings in the appendix. This adds credibility and provides stakeholders with additional perspectives.

Glossary of Terms

Include a glossary of terms used in the monitoring and evaluation section, especially if there are industry-specific or technical terms that may not be familiar to all readers.

References and Citations

If you referred to specific sources or literature in the main text, include a comprehensive list of references and citations in the appendix.

Any Additional Relevant Documents

Include any other documents or materials that provide additional context, evidence, or support for the monitoring and evaluation section. This could vary depending on the specifics of your business and the nature of the evaluation activities.

Remember, while the appendix is a valuable space for additional information, it's essential to maintain clarity and relevance. Only include materials that directly support or enhance the understanding of the content in the main body of the business plan. Including extraneous materials in this section can only lead to confusion.

By addressing all of the components outlined above in the Monitoring and Evaluation section of your business plan, you demonstrate a thoughtful and strategic approach to assessing and improving the performance of your business over time.

13 Supporting Documents

Supporting documents play a vital role in providing credibility and depth to your plan. The specific documents you need may vary based on your industry, business model, and the purpose of the business plan, but this chapter contains some common supporting documents to consider including.

Although you may have already included many of these when writing the sections outlined in previous chapters, you may wish to also make the items outlined below separate documents that you can give to stakeholders, investors, and lenders upon request.

Executive Summary

An executive summary is a concise and compelling overview of a business plan. Despite being one of the first sections in the plan, it is usually the last section written because it summarizes the key points of the entire document. The purpose of an executive summary is to provide a snapshot of your business and its potential, grabbing the reader's attention and encouraging them to delve deeper into the details of the business plan.

Here are the key elements typically included in an executive summary:

Business Name and Location: Clearly state the name and location of your business.

Mission Statement: Briefly describe the purpose and values of your business.

Business Concept: Summarize the nature of your business, including the products or services you offer.

Founding Date and Current Status: Mention when the business was founded and provide a snapshot of its current status.

Ownership Structure: Specify the legal structure of your business (e.g., sole proprietorship, LLC, corporation).

Key Objectives: Outline the primary goals and objectives of your business.

Unique Selling Proposition (USP): Highlight what makes your business unique and sets it apart from competitors.

Target Market: Provide a brief overview of your target market, including demographics and needs.

Financial Summary: Summarize key financial projections, such as sales, profits, and funding requirements.

Key Achievements or Milestones: Highlight any significant accomplishments or milestones your business has achieved.

Management Team: Briefly introduce key members of the management team and their relevant experience.

Funding Request (if applicable): Specify the amount of funding you are seeking and how you plan to use it.

The executive summary is crucial because it serves as the first impression of your business plan. Busy investors or stakeholders may decide whether to read the entire plan based on the strength of the executive summary. Therefore, it is essential to keep it clear, concise, and compelling, providing a snapshot of your business that generates interest and confidence.

Business Description

A well-written business description provides a clear understanding of what your business does, its mission, and its background.

Begin with a brief and engaging introduction that captures the essence of your business. Include fundamental details such as the business name, location, and founding date.

Clearly state your business's mission. Explain the purpose and values that drive your company.

Offer a brief history of your business, emphasizing key milestones and achievements. Highlight how the business evolved to its current state.

Specify the legal structure of your business (e.g., sole proprietorship, LLC, corporation).

Clearly describe the products or services your business offers. Provide enough detail for the reader to understand what sets your offerings apart.

Highlight what makes your business unique and why customers should choose your products or services over competitors.

Identify your target market. Define the demographics, needs, and characteristics of the customers you aim to serve.

Provide a brief overview of your industry. Highlight trends, opportunities, and challenges that may impact your business.

Summarize your business's current status, such as current revenue, customer base, and market share. Outline future plans and goals.

If applicable, mention any key partnerships or relationships that contribute to your business's success.

Briefly discuss your business's adherence to legal and regulatory requirements.

Introduce key members of your management team, highlighting their qualifications and roles.

Provide a snapshot of your financial performance, such as revenue growth, profitability, and any significant financial achievements.

Conclude the business description by discussing your vision for the future and how you plan to achieve your long-term goals.

Remember when writing the business description to keep it as concise as possible. Aim for clarity and brevity. The business description should be succinct and to the point.

Tailor the business description to your audience. Are you writing for investors, lenders, or other stakeholders? Consider the needs and interests of your intended readers (investors, lenders, partners) when crafting your business description.

Remember that the business description sets the tone for the rest of the business plan. It's an opportunity to make a positive first impression and generate interest in your business.

Market Analysis

The market analysis provides an in-depth understanding of the industry, market trends, competition, and your target audience.

Provide a general overview of the industry your business operates in. Include relevant statistics, such as size, growth rate, and major trends.

Mention any external factors (economic, technological, regulatory) that may impact the industry.

Define your target market segment. Specify your target market's demographics, psychographics, and any other relevant characteristics.

Explain the needs and preferences of your target customers. Describe the needs your products or services address in the market. Explain how your offerings fulfill these needs better than or differently from competitors.

Identify and discuss current and future trends in the industry.

Explain how your business can leverage or adapt to these trends.

Provide insights into the growth potential of the market. Include data on historical and projected market growth rates.

Conduct a SWOT analysis (Strengths, Weaknesses, Opportunities, Threats) for your business. Evaluate internal and external factors that may impact your business.

Identify and analyze your key competitors. Assess their strengths, weaknesses, market share, and strategies. Highlight what sets your business apart from competitors (Unique Selling Proposition).

Discuss any barriers that may prevent new competitors from entering the market. This could include high startup costs, access to distribution channels, or established brand loyalty.

Briefly describe the regulatory landscape that affects your industry. Discuss any licenses, permits, or compliance issues relevant to your business.

Outline the stages your customers go through when making a purchase decision. Understand how your business can influence or cater to each stage.

Divide your target market into segments based on common characteristics. Explain how you plan to target and serve each segment.

Analyze how sensitive your target market is to changes in pricing. Consider how your pricing strategy aligns with market expectations.

Describe the channels through which your products or services will reach customers. Consider both traditional and online distribution methods.

Outline your plans for promoting and selling your products or services. Include details about advertising, promotions, and sales tactics.

Identify potential risks in the market that could impact your business. Discuss how you plan to mitigate these risks.

Use a variety of sources for data, including industry reports, market research studies, and interviews with industry experts.

Provide data and statistics to support your statements.

Be realistic and objective in your analysis.

By thoroughly addressing these aspects in your market analysis, you'll provide a clear and well-rounded view of the market conditions, helping potential investors and stakeholders understand the opportunities and challenges your business may face.

Organization and Management

This section is crucial for demonstrating that your business has the necessary talent and leadership to execute your business plan successfully.

Begin by outlining the legal structure of your business (e.g., sole proprietorship, partnership, LLC, corporation). Provide a visual representation of your organizational chart, showing the hierarchy and reporting relationships.

Specify the ownership structure and distribution of shares or ownership percentages among partners, if applicable.

Mention when the business was founded and provide a brief history of its development.

Reiterate the mission and vision of your business, emphasizing how the organizational structure supports these guiding principles.

Introduce the key members of your management team. Include their names, titles, and a brief summary of their roles and responsibilities. Highlight relevant experience, skills, and qualifications that make each team member well-suited for their position.

If applicable, introduce members of the advisory board or board of directors. Provide brief bios highlighting their expertise and roles in advising the company. Clearly define the roles and responsibilities of each key team member. This includes both day-to-day tasks and strategic responsibilities. Ensure that there is clarity about who is responsible for key areas such as finance, marketing, operations, etc.

Address any skills or experience gaps in your current management team. If certain positions are yet to be filled, explain how and when you plan to fill them.

Detail the compensation structure for key team members.

If applicable, explain how ownership or equity is distributed among the management team.

Provide a brief overview of your hiring plan. Mention any key hires that are critical to achieving your business goals in the short or long term.

Outline any plans you have in place for succession, especially if the departure of a key team member could impact the business.

List any external advisors or consultants who play a critical role in supporting your business (e.g., legal counsel, accountants).

Keep your Organization and Management section concise and focused on the most important roles. Avoid unnecessary details. Use visuals, such as organizational charts, to enhance clarity. Demonstrate a balance of skills and experience across your management team.

The Organization and Management section is an opportunity to showcase the qualifications and capabilities of your team, assuring potential investors and stakeholders that your business has the leadership needed to succeed.

Product or Service Line

This section helps potential investors and stakeholders grasp the unique features, benefits, and value propositions of your offerings.

Start with a concise introduction that captures the essence of your products or services.

Clearly state the name of your product(s) and/or service(s).

Provide a high-level overview of what your products or services do.

Emphasize the key problems they solve or the needs they address.

Enumerate the features of your products or services. Explain what sets them apart from alternatives in the market.

Clearly articulate the benefits that customers will derive from using your products or services. Address the pain points your offerings alleviate.

Highlight your Unique Selling Proposition (USP). What makes your products or services stand out from the competition? Why should investors and lenders invest in your business and not one of the others on the market?

Provide technical details and specifications, especially if your products or services have unique technical aspects.

Illustrate the various use cases for your products or services.

Describe how customers can integrate them into their lives or businesses.

Clearly define your target audience for the products or services.

Identify the demographics, characteristics, and preferences of your ideal customers.

Explain how your products or services fulfill specific market needs or trends. Connect your offerings to broader industry demands.

If relevant, describe the development process for your products or services. Discuss any proprietary technologies or intellectual property.

Discuss where your products or services are in their lifecycle. Mention any plans for updates, improvements, or new releases.

Describe how your products are packaged and presented to customers. Consider the visual appeal and branding aspects.

If your products or services need to comply with specific regulations, provide information about how you ensure compliance.

Discuss any plans for future development or expansion of your product or service line. Address how your offerings may evolve to meet changing market needs.

Use visuals like images, diagrams, or prototypes to enhance reader understanding. Tailor the level of technical detail to your audience. Be clear, concise, and avoid jargon that may be unfamiliar to your readers.

By providing a detailed and compelling description of your products or services, you not only inform your audience but also create a persuasive case for the value your offerings bring to the market.

Marketing and Sales

This section is essential for outlining strategies to attract customers, promote your products or services, and generate revenue. Including it as a separate supporting document for your business plan makes it easier for you to distribute to interested parties.

Begin the marketing and sales document with a brief summary of your overall marketing and sales strategy.

Clearly outline your business goals, and specify how marketing and sales efforts will contribute to achieving these goals.

Revisit and expand on the target market information from the market analysis section. Define your ideal customer profiles and demographics.

Reiterate and emphasize your Unique Selling Proposition. What sets your products or services apart from competitors?

Describe how you want your brand to be perceived in the market.

Highlight key messages that communicate your brand's values and benefits.

Outline your pricing strategy. Explain how you've determined your pricing and how it aligns with your overall business strategy.

Detail your distribution strategy. Explain how your products or services will reach customers. Consider both online and offline distribution channels.

Discuss the promotional methods you'll use to reach your target audience. Include online and offline advertising, public relations, content marketing, and social media strategies.

Outline your sales approach, including your sales process and methods for lead generation and conversion.

Specify whether you will use a direct sales force, e-commerce, partnerships, or a combination.

Provide a detailed sales forecast, outlining your expectations for sales over a specific period.

Allocate a budget for your marketing and sales activities. Detail how you plan to allocate funds across various channels and initiatives.

Identify the key metrics and KPIs you'll use to measure the success of your marketing and sales efforts. This could include conversion rates, customer acquisition cost, and return on investment (ROI).

Develop a marketing calendar that outlines the timing of various marketing activities, promotions, and campaigns.

Outline strategies for retaining existing customers, such as loyalty programs, customer support, and follow-up campaigns.

Anticipate potential challenges and outline contingency plans. Discuss how you'll adapt your strategies in response to changes in the market or unexpected events.

Be specific and realistic in your projections and strategies.

Align your marketing and sales plan with your overall business objectives. Regularly update and adapt your plan based on changing market conditions and performance data.

Taking time to develop your marketing and sales plan demonstrates to investors and stakeholders that you have a clear understanding of your target market and a solid strategy for promoting and selling your products or services.

Funding Request

The Funding Request section of a business plan is a critical component and usually the chief reason for writing a business plan in the first place. The Funding Request is where you clearly articulate the amount of funding you are seeking and how you intend to use it.

Whether you are presenting your plan to investors, lenders, or potential partners, it is essential to make a compelling case for why your business needs funding and how it will be utilized.

Start with a concise introduction that states the purpose of the funding request. Mention the total amount of funding you are seeking.

Break down the funding request by specifying how the funds will be used. Provide a detailed allocation of the requested amount. Common categories include product development, marketing, working capital, equipment purchase, or hiring personnel.

Connect the funding request to your financial projections. Explain how the injection of funds will impact your financial performance.

Highlight key metrics such as revenue growth, profitability, and return on investment.

Provide a timeline for when you expect to receive the funding and how it aligns with your business milestones.

Outline when you anticipate achieving specific goals with the allocated funds.

If the funding involves a loan or other forms of repayment, outline your repayment plan. Specify terms, interest rates, and the duration of the repayment period.

If you're seeking equity investment, discuss the potential exit strategies for investors. This might include selling the business, going public, or other scenarios. Acknowledge potential risks associated with the funding request and outline strategies to mitigate those risks. Demonstrate that you've carefully considered the potential challenges. If you're seeking equity funding, provide a clear valuation of your company.

Justify the valuation based on financial performance, market potential, and comparable industry benchmarks.

If your business has received previous funding, provide a brief overview of the history, amounts, and results. Highlight any key achievements or milestones accomplished with previous funding.

Clearly state the terms you are offering to investors, including equity stakes, interest rates, or other relevant terms.

Clearly explain why the requested funding is essential for the growth and success of your business. Emphasize how it will enable you to achieve key objectives and milestones.

Include any additional documents, such as detailed financial models, market research, or legal documents, to support your funding request.

Be realistic and transparent in your funding request. Provide a compelling narrative that aligns your funding needs with your business objectives. Tailor your request to the expectations and requirements of your target audience.

Remember, the Funding Request section is a crucial aspect of your business plan as it directly addresses the financial support needed to implement your business strategy. It's an opportunity to showcase not just the financial need but also the potential return on investment for those considering funding your business.

Financial Projections

Creating projected financial statements such as Income Statements, Balance Sheets, and Cash Flow Statements, is a crucial aspect of a business plan. These statements provide a forecast of your business's financial performance, helping investors and stakeholders understand the anticipated financial health of your company.

Here's a step-by-step guide on how to prepare these projections:

1. Projected Income Statement

   Revenue: List all sources of revenue. Be specific and realistic. Break down revenue by product or service category if applicable.

   Cost of Goods Sold (COGS): Estimate the direct costs associated with producing your goods or services. Include costs such as materials, labor, and manufacturing expenses.

   Gross Profit: Calculate gross profit by subtracting COGS from total revenue.

   Operating Expenses: Itemize operating expenses, including rent, salaries, utilities, marketing, and other overhead costs.

   Categorize expenses as fixed or variable.

   Net Income: Calculate net income by subtracting total operating expenses from gross profit. Provide a net income percentage for context.

2. Projected Balance Sheet

   Assets: List current and non-current assets, including cash, accounts receivable, inventory, equipment, and other assets. Estimate the projected value of each asset.

   Liabilities: List current and long-term liabilities, such as accounts payable, loans, and other debts. Include any deferred revenue or other obligations.

   Equity: Calculate equity by subtracting liabilities from assets. Provide a breakdown of owner's equity.

3. Projected Cash Flow Statement

   Operating Activities: Estimate cash inflows and outflows from day-to-day operations. Include collections from customers, payments to suppliers, salaries, and other operational expenses.

Investing Activities: Include cash transactions related to investments in assets or divestment of assets. This can include purchases of equipment, property, or investments.

Financing Activities: Detail cash flows related to financing, such as loans, equity investments, and dividends. Include any repayments or issuances of debt or equity.

Net Cash Flow: Summarize the net cash flow for each period. Highlight the ending cash balance.

Base your projections on realistic assumptions. Use historical data and market research to inform your estimates.

Break down your projections on a monthly or quarterly basis for the first year and annually for subsequent years. This allows for a more detailed analysis of short-term cash needs.

Consider performing sensitivity analysis by adjusting key assumptions to understand the impact on financial outcomes. This shows that you've considered various scenarios and risks.

Clearly document the assumptions you used to generate your projections. This helps stakeholders understand the basis of your financial forecasts.

If you're not comfortable with financial modeling, consider seeking the help of a financial professional like a Certified Public Accountant or attorney familiar with constructing financial projections. You may also consider using financial software to generate projections. The simpler your business is, the easier it will be for you to do it yourself. For more complicated financial projections it is better to rely on professionals. Doing so demonstrates your commitment to excellence.

This is an example of how to construct a simple projected income statement. You can create it using a spreadsheet software like Excel.

Projected Income Statement (Year 1)

REVENUE	$XXX,XXX.XX
Cost of Goods Sold (COGS)	$XX,XXX.XX
Gross Profit	$XX,XXX.XX
Operating Expenses	$XX,XXX.XX
Net Income	$XX,XXX.XX

Projected Balance Sheet (End of Year 1)

ASSETS	$X,XXX.XX	LIABILITIES	$X,XXX.XX	EQUITY	$X,XXX.XX
Cash	$X,XXX.XX	Accounts Payable	$X,XXX.XX	Owner Equity	$X,XXX.XX
Inventory	$X,XXX.XX	Loans Payable	$X,XXX.XX		
Equipment	$X,XXX.XX				

Projected Cash Flow Statement (Year 1)

Operating Activities	$XXX,XXX.XX
Investing Activities	$XXX,XXX.XX
Financing Activities	$XXX,XXX.XX
Net Cash Flow	$XXX,XXX.XX

The accuracy and transparency of your financial projections are crucial for building trust with investors and stakeholders. Regularly update your projections based on actual performance, and be prepared to explain and justify your assumptions during discussions with potential investors or lenders.

Legal Structure and Compliance:

The Legal Structure and Compliance document is an important part of the supporting documents section in your business plan. This section provides detailed information about the legal framework within which your business operates and ensures compliance with relevant laws and regulations.

Here is how you can structure and write this document:

1. Legal Structure

Business Entity Type: Clearly state the legal structure of your business (e.g., sole proprietorship, partnership, LLC, corporation). Explain why the chosen structure is suitable for your business.

Ownership Details: Provide details about the ownership structure, including the names and ownership percentages of partners or shareholders. If applicable, outline any plans for changes in ownership.

Registered Business Name: Include the registered business name and any trade names or DBAs (Doing Business As) that you use.

Registered Agent: Identify the registered agent if required by your legal structure. Explain the agent's role in receiving legal documents on behalf of the business.

Articles of Incorporation or Organization: If your business is a corporation or an LLC, include details from your articles of incorporation or organization.

Operating Agreement or Bylaws: Provide information on the operating agreement (for an LLC) or bylaws (for a corporation). Highlight key provisions related to ownership, management, and decision-making.

2. Regulatory Compliance

Industry-specific Regulations: Outline the industry-specific regulations that your business must comply with. Explain how you ensure adherence to these regulations.

Licensing and Permits: List all necessary licenses and permits required for your business operations. Include details about the application status, renewal dates, and compliance history.

Local, State, and Federal Regulations: Describe how your business complies with local, state, and federal laws and regulations. Include information about taxes, labor laws, environmental regulations, etc.

3. Intellectual Property

Trademarks, Patents, and Copyrights: If applicable, detail any trademarks, patents, or copyrights associated with your products or services. Include registration numbers and expiration dates.

Protection Strategies: Outline strategies for protecting your intellectual property. This could include confidentiality agreements, non-disclosure agreements, and other protective measures.

4. Contracts and Agreements

Key Contracts: List and briefly describe key contracts and agreements your business is a party to. Include details such as partners, vendors, suppliers, and clients.

Terms and Conditions: If your business has an online presence, provide terms and conditions for website usage, if applicable. Include privacy policies and any other legal notices.

5. Compliance Monitoring

Compliance Officer or Team: If applicable, identify the person or team responsible for monitoring compliance. Explain their roles and responsibilities.

Compliance Monitoring Procedures: Provide an overview of your compliance monitoring procedures. Explain how you stay informed about changes in regulations.

Be transparent and thorough in providing information about your legal structure and compliance efforts. Seek legal advice where necessary to ensure accuracy and completeness. Regularly update this document to reflect any changes in your business structure or regulatory environment.

The Legal Structure and Compliance document not only provides assurance to stakeholders about your commitment to legal and regulatory standards but also helps build trust and credibility for your business.

Risk Analysis

A Risk Analysis document is necessary for identifying, assessing, and managing potential risks that could impact the success of your business. This section demonstrates your awareness of potential challenges and your proactive approach to mitigating these risks. Start with an introduction that provides context for the risk analysis. Explain the importance of identifying and mitigating risks for the success of the business.

Clearly define the scope of the risk analysis. Specify whether you're focusing on internal or external risks, industry-specific risks, or broader economic factors.

Identify and categorize potential risks. Common categories include operational, financial, market, legal, regulatory, and strategic risks.

Specify the sources of risks, such as industry trends, economic conditions, technological changes, competition, and internal operational factors. List specific events or scenarios that could lead to negative outcomes. Include both internal and external factors that may contribute to risk events.

Assess the likelihood of each identified risk occurring and the potential impact on your business. Use a scale (e.g., low, medium, high) to quantify likelihood and impact.

Create a risk matrix that visualizes the relationship between likelihood and impact. Classify risks into categories such as high priority, medium priority, and low priority.

Highlight critical risks that have high likelihood and high impact.

Prioritize these risks for detailed mitigation planning.

Develop detailed mitigation plans for critical risks. Specify actions, responsibilities, and timelines for implementing mitigation strategies.

Outline contingency plans for each identified risk. Describe the steps you'll take if a risk materializes. Describe the mechanisms you'll use to monitor and track risks. This could include regular reviews, key performance indicators, and early warning systems. Specify how often you'll review and update the risk analysis.

Regularly revisit and adjust the analysis as the business environment evolves.

Discuss any insurance coverage in place to mitigate certain risks.

Specify the types of coverage and coverage limits.

If applicable, mention contractual agreements that transfer or share certain risks with third parties. Include details of indemnification clauses and risk allocation strategies.

Outline how you'll communicate risks and mitigation strategies to internal and external stakeholders. Establish clear lines of communication for handling and reporting risks.

Be comprehensive in your identification of risks, considering both internal and external factors. Involve key stakeholders, including management and subject matter experts, in the risk analysis process.

Keep the language clear and avoid jargon to ensure understanding by all readers.

A well-drafted Risk Analysis document demonstrates your commitment to thorough business planning and risk management. It provides valuable insights for potential investors and stakeholders into how you're prepared to handle challenges and uncertainties that may arise during the course of your business operations.

Operational Plan

The Operational Plan document outlines the day-to-day processes and procedures that are essential for running the business. This section provides details on how your business will function, covering areas such as production, facilities, equipment, personnel, and more. It should have been included in a separate section in your business plan, but if you choose to create a simplified version for your supporting documents, it may help your readers quickly summarize the operations of your business. When creating such a document you may wish to do so in outline or bullet point form.

Here is a step-by-step guide on how to do so:

Begin with a brief introduction that summarizes your business and its main operations. Highlight the key objectives of the operational plan.

Clearly define the scope of the operational plan, specifying which aspects of the business operations will be covered.

Provide details about the physical location of your business, including address, size, and any special features. If applicable, include information about multiple locations.

Describe the facilities, equipment, and technology infrastructure required for your operations. Mention any plans for expansion or upgrades.

Outline the step-by-step process involved in producing your products or delivering your services. Include details about the materials, equipment, and technology used.

Discuss the measures in place to ensure the quality and consistency of your products or services. Highlight any certifications or quality standards your business adheres to.

Describe how you will manage inventory, including ordering, receiving, storage, and tracking. Mention any software or technology used for inventory management.

Detail relationships with suppliers, including terms, agreements, and backup plans in case of supply chain disruptions.

Provide an organizational chart detailing the hierarchy of positions and reporting relationships. Include the names and roles of key personnel.

Define the roles and responsibilities of each team member. Clarify reporting lines and communication channels.

Outline plans for employee training and development. Mention any ongoing training programs to enhance skills.

Explain how your operations comply with local, state, and federal regulations. Include any industry-specific compliance requirements.

List and provide details about the permits and licenses necessary for your operations. Include expiration dates and renewal processes.

Detail the technology infrastructure supporting your operations, including hardware, software, and networks. Highlight any cybersecurity measures.

Discuss any automation tools or systems implemented to enhance operational efficiency. Mention plans for future technology upgrades.

Identify potential operational risks and challenges. Discuss strategies for mitigating and managing these risks.

Outline contingency plans for various operational scenarios. Include details on how the business will adapt to unforeseen challenges.

Define the Key Performance Indicators (KPIs) that will be used to measure the success of your operations.

Explain how you will monitor and evaluate operational performance.

Specify the frequency of reviews and adjustments.

Use clear and concise language to enhance readability. Align the operational plan with the overall business goals and objectives.

Regularly update the operational plan as your business evolves.

By providing a comprehensive overview of your business's day-to-day operations, the Operational Plan document assures stakeholders and investors that you have a well-thought-out strategy for managing resources and delivering products or services efficiently.

Exit Strategy:

The Exit Strategy document outlines the planned exit options for the business owners or investors. While not every business plan requires a detailed exit strategy, it is a critical component for those seeking investment or partnerships. It lets investors know when and how an exit will or should take place. If you decide to include this supporting document in your business plan, you will want to include the information outlined below.

Begin with a brief introduction explaining the purpose of the exit strategy. Clarify that it provides a roadmap for potential exits for investors or business owners.

Mention when the exit strategy is likely to be executed, such as after a certain period or achievement of specific milestones.

Outline the possibility of selling the entire business to another company or an interested buyer. Specify potential acquirers or industries that might be interested.

Discuss the option of taking the company public through an IPO (Initial Public Offering). Highlight the advantages and challenges associated with this approach.

Explore the possibility of merging with another company or being acquired. Discuss potential synergies and benefits for both parties.

Explain the options for the management team or employees to buy the business through things like a Management Buyout (MBO) or Employee Stock Ownership Plan (ESOP). Outline the benefits, the risks, and the steps involved.

Address the possibility of liquidating the business if no other viable options are available. Detail how assets would be sold and liabilities settled.

Discuss how the business will be valued for the purpose of the exit. Explain the methods and factors that will be considered.

Specify when and how often the business will be valued, especially if the exit is tied to specific milestones or events.

Identify specific financial milestones that may trigger the consideration of an exit. For example, reaching a certain level of revenue or profitability.

Discuss how market conditions may influence the decision to exit. Consider trends in the industry and economic conditions.

Acknowledge that personal circumstances of the business owner(s) may also be a factor in the decision to exit. This could include retirement, health issues, or a desire for a career change.

Outline how stakeholders will be informed about the decision to exit. Consider communication with employees, customers, suppliers, and investors.

Specify when and how the decision to exit will be communicated. Include any provisions for confidentiality.

Ensure that the exit strategy complies with legal and regulatory requirements. Address any legal obligations to shareholders or employees.

Review existing contracts and agreements to ensure that the exit plan aligns with their terms. Consider any change-of-control provisions.

Be realistic and transparent about the potential exit options. Tailor the exit strategy to the specific circumstances of your business. Regularly review and update the exit strategy as business conditions evolve.

An Exit Strategy document provides clarity for investors and stakeholders about the potential outcomes and financial returns associated with their involvement in the business. It is a proactive step that demonstrates careful consideration of the long-term trajectory of the company, therefore most investors and lenders will be looking at your business plan to see if your exit strategy has been carefully planned.

Appendix

This is the section where you would include any additional information that supports your business plan.

Examples of supporting information to add to this section include:

- Market research data.
- Legal documents (contracts, licenses, permits).
- Letters of support or endorsements.
- Relevant photos, charts, graphs, or other visuals.

Always tailor the supporting documents to the specific needs of your business and your audience. Providing thorough and accurate information helps build confidence among potential investors, partners, and other stakeholders.

14 Additional Financial Information

When writing a business plan, providing comprehensive and well-thought-out financial information is crucial for demonstrating the viability and potential success of your business. Although we have gone over some of the information in this chapter in other sections of this book, here we'll be doing a deep-dive to make sure your business plan contains critical financial information that investors, lenders, and other stakeholders will be looking for.

Most of the financial information investors will be looking for is discussed in the chapter on writing your Financial Plan; however, there are some types of financial information that are optional for some businesses. Writing any business plan is a delicate balancing act between being comprehensive and being redundant, so it's up to you to decide how much of the information in this chapter is relevant to your own venture's business, and to plan accordingly.

The financial information discussed in this chapter is optional for some businesses, but a necessity for other businesses. If you are unsure about whether or not you should include the information in this chapter in your own business plan, solicit feedback from your stakeholders prior to including it.

Expense Budget

Creating an expense budget for your business plan involves estimating the costs associated with operating your business. A budget helps you understand your financial needs and demonstrates to investors and stakeholders that you have a clear understanding of your organization's financial requirements.

Start by listing major expense categories relevant to your business.

Common categories include:

Fixed Expenses: Rent, salaries, insurance, utilities, subscriptions, and loan repayments.

Variable Expenses: Raw materials, production costs, marketing, travel, and sales-related expenses.

Gather accurate and up-to-date information for each expense category. Use quotes, invoices, market research, or industry benchmarks to support your estimates.

Distinguish between fixed and variable costs. Fixed costs remain constant regardless of production levels, while variable costs fluctuate with business activity.

Break down your annual expenses into monthly estimates. Some expenses, like rent and salaries, are usually fixed and easy to allocate on a monthly basis. Variable expenses may require more detailed projections based on sales forecasts.

If your business experiences seasonal fluctuations, account for these variations in your expense budget. Adjust your estimates accordingly to reflect peak and off-peak periods.

Account for any one-time or startup expenses, such as legal fees, permits, licenses, equipment purchases, or initial marketing costs.

Add a contingency fund to cover unexpected expenses or cost overruns. A common practice is to set aside 5-10% of the total budget for contingencies.

Organize your expense budget in a spreadsheet or accounting software. This makes it easier to update, track, and analyze your financial data.

Include detailed descriptions for each expense item. This helps readers understand the purpose of each cost and demonstrates transparency.

Regularly review and update your expense budget as your business evolves. Adjust your projections based on actual performance and any changes in the business environment.

Ensure that your expense budget aligns with your overall business goals and strategies. Prioritize spending in areas that contribute most to your venture's success.

After your business is operational, compare actual expenses to your budgeted amounts regularly. This will help you identify any variances and adjust your budget accordingly.

Clearly communicate the assumptions underlying your expense budget. If certain costs are based on estimates or industry averages, make this clear to your audience.

If you're unsure about certain expenses or need assistance, consider consulting with a financial advisor or accountant to ensure accuracy and completeness.

Break-even Analysis

A break-even analysis helps you determine the point at which your business becomes profitable and covers all its costs.

Start by categorizing your costs into fixed and variable. Fixed costs remain constant regardless of production levels (e.g., rent, salaries), while variable costs fluctuate with production or sales (e.g., raw materials, direct labor).

Set the selling price for your product or service. This is the price at which you will sell each unit.

Contribution margin is the *selling price per unit* minus the *variable cost per unit*. It represents the portion of each sale that contributes to covering fixed costs and profit.

The formula is:

$$\text{Contribution Margin} = \text{Selling Price} - \text{Variable Cost per Unit}$$

Identify your total fixed costs. These are the costs that do not change with the level of production.

Use this formula to find the break-even point in units:

$$\text{Break-even Point (in units)} = \frac{\text{Fixed Costs}}{\text{Contribution Margin per Unit}}$$

Next, determine the break-even point in terms of revenue:

$$\text{Break-Even Point (in revenue)} = \text{Break-Even Point (in units)} \times \text{Selling Price}$$

Create a break-even chart to visually represent the relationship between costs, revenue, and profit. The break-even point is where the total revenue and total cost lines intersect.

Conduct sensitivity analysis by considering different scenarios. For example, explore how changes in selling price or variable costs affect the break-even point.

Integrate the break-even analysis into your business plan if your research indicates that this is something your stakeholders would require to be included. Provide a clear explanation of the methodology and assumptions used in calculating the break-even point.

Interpret the break-even results. Discuss what the break-even point means for your business, how many units or dollars you need to sell to cover costs, and the significance of reaching profitability.

Compare your break-even point to your sales projections. This helps you assess the feasibility of your business plan and set realistic sales targets.

Periodically revisit and update your break-even analysis as your business evolves. Changes in costs, pricing, or market conditions may impact your break-even point.

While break-even analysis focuses on covering costs, it is important to consider cash flow. Even if you break even, you need to ensure that you have sufficient cash to cover day-to-day operations.

A well-executed break-even analysis provides insights into the financial health of your business and helps you and your stakeholders make informed decisions about pricing, cost management, and overall strategy. It is an essential tool for both business planning and ongoing financial management.

Funding Requirements

The funding requirements section of your business plan outlines the financial needs of your business and provides details on how much capital you are seeking and how you plan to use it. You can include it in the Financial Plan section if you wish, but making it a separate section can make it stand out, and make it easier for lenders and investors to know what you're asking for and why.

section with a brief executive summary that highlights the amount of funding you are seeking and the key purposes for which the funds will be used.

Provide a detailed breakdown of the funding you are seeking. Specify the total amount of funding required and the type of funding you are seeking (e.g., equity investment, debt financing, a combination of both).

Clearly outline how you plan to allocate the funds. Specify the purpose of each portion of the funding, such as:

- Startup costs (e.g., equipment, initial inventory, legal fees).
- Working capital for day-to-day operations.
- Marketing and advertising expenses.
- Research and development costs.
- Expansion or growth initiatives.

Provide a timeline for when you anticipate needing the funds and how you plan to utilize them over time. This helps demonstrate that you have a well-thought-out plan for managing your cash flow.

Justify why the funding is necessary for your business. Highlight key milestones or achievements that the funding will enable, and explain how it contributes to the overall success and growth of the business. Don't neglect this section, as it is crucial to lenders and investors in determining whether or not to invest in your business.

Tie the funding requirements to your financial projections. Show how the infusion of capital will impact your revenue, expenses, and overall financial performance.

If you're seeking equity investment, discuss the expected ROI for investors. Highlight the potential for investors to realize a profitable return on their investment in your business.

If seeking equity investment, briefly mention your exit strategy. Explain how investors can expect to realize a return on their investment, whether through an IPO, acquisition, or other means.

Acknowledge potential risks and challenges associated with your funding requirements. Demonstrate that you have considered potential obstacles and have strategies in place to mitigate risks.

Address any legal or regulatory requirements related to the funding you are seeking. Be transparent about how you plan to comply with relevant laws and regulations.

If you are seeking a loan, outline your repayment plan. Specify the terms, interest rates, and the anticipated timeline for repaying the loan.

If the funding requires collateral, clearly identify the assets you are willing to pledge and their estimated value.

Seek professional advice if needed, especially when dealing with complex funding structures or legal requirements. Consult with financial advisors, attorneys, or accountants to ensure accuracy and compliance.

Include any supporting documents, such as financial statements, market research, or legal documents, in the appendix to provide additional context for your funding requirements.

Remember to tailor the funding requirements section to your specific business and the needs of your audience, whether it is potential investors, lenders, or other stakeholders. Be transparent, realistic, and thorough in presenting your financial needs and plans.

Financial Assumptions

The financial assumptions section outlines the key assumptions you have made in preparing your financial projections. While most businesses include this in the Financial Plan section of the business plan, there are some who choose to include it as a separate section.

It provides transparency to readers, such as investors or stakeholders, about the basis for your financial forecasts.

Begin with a brief introduction to the financial assumptions section, emphasizing the importance of transparency and the role that assumptions play in financial forecasting.

Start by detailing the assumptions related to your revenue projections. Include factors such as:

- Pricing strategy.
- Sales volume growth rates.

- Market share assumptions.
- Assumptions about the demand for your product or service.

Outline the assumptions regarding your cost of goods sold, which includes the direct costs associated with producing your product or delivering your service. This may include:

- Raw material costs.
- Manufacturing costs.
- Direct labor costs.
- Any expected changes in these costs over time.

Specify the assumptions related to operating expenses, which encompass the day-to-day costs of running your business. This could involve:

- Rent and utilities.
- Salaries and benefits.
- Marketing and advertising expenses.
- Administrative costs.
- Any assumptions about changes in these expenses.

If your business requires significant capital expenditures, outline the assumptions related to these investments. This might include:

- Equipment purchases.
- Facility upgrades.
- Technology investments.
- The timing and scale of these expenditures.

Address assumptions related to working capital, which involves the funds needed to cover day-to-day operational expenses. Key elements may include:

- Inventory levels and turnover.
- Accounts receivable and payable.
- Cash flow cycles and any expected changes.

If applicable, include assumptions related to interest expenses and taxes. This could involve:

- Interest rates on loans.
- Tax rates and any tax incentives.
- Changes in interest or tax rates over time.

If your business operates in multiple currencies or regions, address assumptions related to currency exchange rates and inflation rates. This is particularly important for international businesses.

Consider external factors that may impact your financial projections. Include assumptions related to:

- Market trends and conditions.

- Economic indicators.
- Industry-specific factors.

Acknowledge potential risks and uncertainties associated with your assumptions. Discuss contingency plans or alternative scenarios you've considered to address these risks.

Ensure that your assumptions are consistent with each other and rational. Avoid making overly optimistic or unrealistic assumptions that may undermine the credibility of your financial projections.

Document the sources of your assumptions and provide references to any market research, industry data, or expert opinions that support your assumptions.

Emphasize that assumptions should be regularly reviewed and updated based on changes in the business environment, market conditions, or other relevant factors.

By clearly articulating your financial assumptions, you provide transparency and allow readers to understand the foundation of your financial projections. This section helps build confidence in the credibility of your business plan and financial forecasts.

Financial Ratios

Explaining financial ratios in a business plan is essential for helping readers understand the financial health and performance of your company. Financial ratios provide insights into various aspects of your business, such as profitability, liquidity, solvency, and efficiency.

Start by providing a brief introduction to the concept of financial ratios. Explain that ratios are quantitative indicators that help assess different aspects of your organization's financial performance.

Categorize financial ratios into relevant groups. Common categories include:

Profitability Ratios: Measure the company's ability to generate profits.

Liquidity Ratios: Assess the company's ability to meet short-term obligations.

Solvency Ratios: Evaluate the company's long-term financial stability.

Efficiency Ratios: Measure how effectively the company utilizes its assets.

For each ratio you include in your business plan, provide a clear explanation of what it measures and why it is relevant. Some examples include:

Return on Investment (ROI): This ratio shows how efficiently the company generates profits relative to its investment. A higher ROI is generally favorable.

Current Ratio: This liquidity ratio indicates the company's ability to cover short-term liabilities with its short-term assets. A ratio above 1 indicates a healthy liquidity position.

Debt-to-Equity Ratio: A solvency ratio that shows the proportion of debt used to finance the company's assets compared to equity. Lower ratios are often considered more favorable.

Include the formula for each ratio to provide a clear understanding of how it is calculated. For example:

Return on Investment:

$$ROI = \left(\frac{\text{Net Profit}}{\text{Total Investment}} \right) \times 100$$

Current Ratio:

$$\text{Current Ratio} = \frac{\text{Current Assets}}{\text{Current Liabilities}}$$

Debt-to-Equity Ratio:

$$\text{Debt-to-Equity Ratio} = \frac{\text{Current Debt}}{\text{Current Equity}}$$

Compare your financial ratios to industry benchmarks or standards to provide context. If your ratios deviate significantly from industry norms, explain the reasons for the variance and any steps you're taking to address it.

Include trend analysis by presenting historical data for each ratio. Discuss how these ratios have evolved over time and the factors that contributed to the changes.

Interpret the results of each ratio and discuss their implications for your business. For example, a declining profitability ratio may prompt a discussion about cost management strategies.

Explain how you use financial ratios for internal decision-making.

Discuss how these ratios inform your strategic planning, budgeting, and overall financial management.

Acknowledge any limitations or potential risks associated with relying solely on financial ratios. Discuss the importance of considering other qualitative and contextual factors.

Consider incorporating charts or graphs to visually represent the trend and comparative analysis of key financial ratios. Visuals can enhance clarity and make complex information more accessible.

Discuss how changes in key assumptions or external factors might impact your financial ratios. This demonstrates a forward-looking approach to financial management.

Include any supporting documentation, such as detailed financial statements or calculations, in the appendix of your business plan for readers who want to delve deeper into the numbers.

By providing a comprehensive and well-explained overview of financial ratios, you demonstrate a strong understanding of your venture's financial performance and instill confidence in your readers, whether they are potential investors, lenders, or other stakeholders.

Contingency Plans

Addressing potential financial risks and uncertainties in a business plan is a crucial aspect of demonstrating thorough planning and risk management.

Start by identifying potential financial risks and uncertainties that could impact your business. These could include market fluctuations, economic downturns, changes in regulations, supplier issues, competition, and more.

Categorize identified risks into different categories, such as market risks, operational risks, financial risks, regulatory risks, and external risks. This helps in organizing and prioritizing your risk management efforts.

Provide a quantitative and qualitative assessment of each identified risk. Quantify the potential financial impact and likelihood of occurrence where possible. This helps prioritize risks based on their severity.

For each identified risk, outline specific strategies for mitigating or reducing its impact. Strategies may include diversification, contingency planning, insurance, contract negotiations, or developing alternative suppliers.

Develop contingency plans for high-impact risks. Clearly outline the steps your business will take in response to specific adverse events, such as a sudden drop in sales or an unexpected increase in production costs.

Conduct stress tests on your financial projections. Assess how changes in key variables (e.g., sales, costs, interest rates) would impact your financial performance. This helps identify vulnerabilities and areas that may require additional attention.

Perform scenario analysis by considering different economic or market scenarios. Evaluate the impact of both optimistic and pessimistic scenarios on your financial outcomes. This provides a more comprehensive view of potential risks.

Allocate a portion of your budget as a buffer or reserve fund to absorb unexpected costs or revenue shortfalls. This can act as a financial cushion during challenging times.

Evaluate the need for insurance coverage to protect against specific risks. This might include business interruption insurance, liability insurance, or other forms of coverage that are relevant to your industry.

Strengthen relationships with key suppliers and customers. Collaborate closely with suppliers to ensure a stable supply chain, and maintain good communication with customers to understand their needs and potential changes in demand.

Schedule regular reviews of your risk management plan. As your business evolves and market conditions change, update your risk assessments and adjust mitigation strategies accordingly.

Highlight the adaptability and flexibility of your financial strategy. Explain how your business can pivot or adjust its operations in response to changing conditions, whether it's a shift in consumer preferences or unexpected economic challenges.

Develop a communication plan for stakeholders in the event of significant risks materializing. Transparent communication fosters trust, and having a plan in place demonstrates that your business is prepared to handle challenges.

Stay informed about changes in regulations that may impact your business. Ensure that your financial strategy includes compliance measures to address regulatory risks.

Consider seeking advice from financial experts, consultants, or industry specialists. External perspectives can provide valuable insights into potential risks and effective mitigation strategies.

By thoroughly addressing financial risks and uncertainties in your business plan, you not only demonstrate a realistic understanding of potential challenges but also showcase your proactive approach to risk management. This can instill confidence in stakeholders, including investors, lenders, and partners.

The financial section of your business plan should be well-researched, realistic, and supported by data and market analysis. It is a crucial tool for convincing potential investors, lenders, and stakeholders of your business's financial viability and potential for success.

15 LEGAL DOCUMENTS

Including key legal documents in a business plan is important as it provides transparency, helps build trust with stakeholders, and demonstrates that your business is operating within legal boundaries.

While the specific legal documents may vary based on your industry, business structure, and location, here are some common ones to consider including in your business plan:

Business Structure Documents

Some types of business structure documents to consider including in your business plan:

Articles of Incorporation/Formation: For corporations or LLCs, include the document filed with the state that officially establishes the business.

Partnership Agreement: If your business is a partnership, provide the partnership agreement that outlines the terms and conditions agreed upon by partners.

Ownership and Equity Documents

Some types of ownership and equity documents to consider including in your business plan:

Shareholder Agreement: For corporations, this document outlines the rights and responsibilities of shareholders, including issues related to ownership, voting, and transfer of shares.

Operating Agreement: For LLCs, this document specifies the roles, responsibilities, and rights of members and details how the business will be managed.

Intellectual Property Documents

Some types of intellectual property documents to consider including in your business plan:

Patents, Trademarks, and Copyrights: Include documentation related to any patents, trademarks, or copyrights your business owns. This can demonstrate the uniqueness and protectability of your products or services.

Contracts and Agreements

Some types of contracts and agreements documents to consider including in your business plan:

Client Contracts: Include sample contracts or templates for agreements with clients or customers, detailing terms, deliverables, payment terms, and other important provisions.

Supplier Agreements: Provide documentation related to agreements with suppliers, outlining terms of procurement, pricing, and other key conditions.

Employee Contracts: If applicable, include employment contracts or offer letters outlining terms of employment, responsibilities, compensation, and benefits.

Regulatory Compliance Documents

Some types of regulatory compliance documents to consider including in your business plan:

Business Licenses and Permits: Include copies of any required business licenses and permits to demonstrate that your business is operating legally within regulatory frameworks.

Compliance Plans: Detail any compliance plans your business has in place to adhere to industry-specific regulations or standards.

Financial Documents

Some types of financial documents to consider including in your business plan:

Financial Statements: Include audited or reviewed financial statements, such as balance sheets, income statements, and cash flow statements, to provide a clear picture of your business's financial health.

Tax Returns: Include recent tax returns to demonstrate compliance with tax obligations.

Leases and Real Estate Documents

Some types of leases and real estate documents to consider including in your business plan:

Lease Agreements: Include copies of lease agreements for business premises or equipment. This is particularly important if the physical location is a critical aspect of your business.

Property Titles: Include copies of titles for real estate owned by the business. This is particularly important if seeking equity loans for funding.

Insurance Policies

Provide information on the types of insurance coverage your business holds, such as general liability, property, or professional liability insurance.

Dispute Resolution Documents

Include documentation related to dispute resolution mechanisms, such as arbitration or mediation agreements, to demonstrate how conflicts will be resolved.

Confidentiality and Non-Disclosure Agreements

If your business relies on proprietary information, include copies of NDAs you use to protect sensitive information when sharing it with employees, contractors, or partners.

Exit Strategy Documents

For businesses with multiple owners, include buy-sell agreements that outline the process for selling or transferring ownership interests.

Compliance with Environmental Regulations

If applicable, include documentation related to your business's compliance with environmental regulations.

Including these legal documents in your business plan provides a comprehensive overview of the legal structure, operations, and risk management practices of your business. It also reassures investors, lenders, and other stakeholders that your business is well-organized and compliant with legal requirements. Keep in mind that while providing relevant documents, you should also be mindful of confidentiality and privacy concerns. Balance the need to inform your readers with the need for privacy and security.

16 Conclusion and Resources

Writing an effective business plan is both an art and a science. Through the journey of this book, we've explored the essential elements, strategic considerations, and practical insights needed to create a roadmap for business success. Writing a business plan is not merely a box to check; it's a dynamic process that demands careful research, thoughtful analysis, and a clear vision of the future. It also requires constant updating on at least a quarterly basis.

As you embark on your entrepreneurial journey armed with the knowledge and tools provided in these pages, remember that a business plan is more than a document—it is a living, breathing guide that evolves with your business. Regularly revisit and update your plan, adapting it to changing market conditions, new opportunities, and unexpected challenges.

Successful business plans are born from a deep understanding of your industry, a realistic assessment of your strengths and weaknesses, and a commitment to continuous improvement. Embrace feedback, stay resilient in the face of uncertainties, and be open to refining your strategies as your business journey unfolds.

Your business plan should be a compass that guides you through uncharted territories, a strategic weapon that helps you navigate challenges, and a persuasive tool that attracts the support of investors, lenders, and partners. With a well-crafted business plan in hand, you are not just outlining a vision. You are setting the stage for the realization of your entrepreneurial dreams.

Remember that the journey of entrepreneurship is a marathon, not a sprint. Your business plan is your trusted companion on this race, providing direction, purpose, and a framework for success. Look forward to the adventure ahead, the challenges you will conquer, and the milestones that await on the path to building a thriving and sustainable business.

Resources

Writing a business plan requires careful research, analysis, and strategic thinking. Here are some resources that can help you in the process of creating a comprehensive and effective business plan.

U.S. Small Business Administration (SBA)

The SBA offers a variety of resources, including guides and templates, to help entrepreneurs develop their business plans. The SBA website provides step-by-step instructions and advice.

SCORE

SCORE is a nonprofit organization that provides free mentoring and resources to small businesses. They offer business plan templates, workshops, and online resources to guide you through the planning process.

Bplans

Bplans is an online resource that offers a wide range of free sample business plans and templates. It covers various industries and can serve as a helpful reference for structuring your own business plan.

LivePlan

LivePlan is a paid business planning tool that provides step-by-step guidance and a user-friendly interface. It helps you create financial projections, conduct market analysis, and develop a polished business plan.

Small Business Development Centers (SBDCs)

SBDCs, often affiliated with universities and colleges, offer free or low-cost business consulting services. They can provide guidance on business planning and connect you with local resources.

Books on Business Planning

There are many books dedicated to the art of business planning. Some recommended titles include "Business Model Generation" by Alexander Osterwalder and Yves Pigneur, and "The Lean Startup" by Eric Ries.

Entrepreneurial Websites and Magazines

Websites like Entrepreneur.com and Inc.com provide a wealth of articles, guides, and tools related to business planning. Entrepreneurial magazines, such as Inc. Magazine, often feature business plan insights and success stories.

Chambers of Commerce

Local Chambers of Commerce may offer workshops or resources to help entrepreneurs develop their business plans. They can also connect you with local business support networks.

Your Local Library

Many libraries offer access to business planning books, industry reports, and online databases. Librarians can be valuable resources for finding relevant information and research materials.

Online Courses and Webinars

Platforms like Coursera, Udemy, and edX offer online courses on business planning and entrepreneurship. These courses may cover topics such as market analysis, financial modeling, and strategic planning.

Business Plan Competitions

Participating in business plan competitions, either locally or nationally, can provide valuable feedback and mentorship. Look for competitions hosted by universities, organizations, or entrepreneurial events.

Industry Associations and Trade Publications

Industry-specific associations often provide resources and insights relevant to business planning. Additionally, trade publications within your industry may offer case studies and market analysis.

Government Resources

Check government websites for resources specific to your country or region. In addition to the SBA in the U.S., government agencies often provide guides and information for small businesses.

Remember that while these resources can be valuable guides, it's essential to tailor your business plan to your specific industry, target audience, and business model. Be thorough in your research, and seek feedback from mentors, industry experts, and other entrepreneurs as you develop your business plan.

Best of luck on your entrepreneurial journey, and may your business plan be the catalyst for turning your dreams into reality.

Appendices

APPENDIX A:

Understanding and Utilizing Product Life Cycles in Business Planning

The concept of a product life cycle (PLC) is a fundamental element in strategic business planning, guiding companies through the stages of a product's existence from introduction to decline. Recognizing and understanding these stages is crucial for businesses seeking sustained success, enabling effective decision-making and resource allocation. It is important to understand the significance of product life cycles in the context of a business plan, outlining the stages and strategies associated with each phase.

Stages of the Product Life Cycle

At the onset, a product is introduced to the market. Sales are typically slow as consumers become familiar with the offering. Initial investment focuses on research and development, market research, and promotion to create awareness.

Growth

During this phase, consumer acceptance grows, leading to an uptick in sales. Competitors may enter the market, prompting increased marketing efforts and distribution expansion. Profits begin to rise as economies of scale are realized.

Maturity

In the maturity stage, sales peak, and competition intensifies. Pricing becomes a critical factor, and businesses often focus on product differentiation and cost efficiencies. Marketing efforts shift from creating awareness to maintaining market share.

Decline

Eventually, every product faces a decline as consumer interest wanes, often due to changing trends, technological advancements, or shifting consumer preferences. Companies must decide whether to phase out the product, modify it, or explore new markets.

Significance of PLC in Business Planning

There are multiple reasons to consider the Product Life Cycle when writing a business plan. Some of these include:

Strategic Decision-Making: Recognizing the product life cycle assists in making informed strategic decisions. In the introduction stage, businesses may prioritize innovation and differentiation, while in maturity, focus shifts to cost control and sustaining market share.

Resource Allocation: Efficient allocation of resources is paramount. In the growth stage, additional investments may be required to capitalize on the expanding market. Conversely, during decline, resources may be redirected to newer products or markets.

Marketing and Promotion: Marketing strategies evolve with each stage. In the introduction phase, emphasis is on creating awareness, while the growth phase requires promotional efforts to capture a broader audience. Maturity demands brand maintenance, and the decline stage necessitates thoughtful promotion for repositioning or liquidation.

Risk Management: Understanding the product life cycle aids in risk assessment. Businesses can anticipate and mitigate risks associated with market saturation, competition, or technological advancements by planning for potential challenges at each stage.

Innovation and Adaptation: As products move through the life cycle, innovation becomes vital. Businesses must continually adapt products to meet changing consumer needs, technological advancements, or market trends to stay relevant and competitive.

Financial Planning: Financial forecasts are heavily influenced by the product life cycle. Businesses must anticipate the need for initial investments during introduction, increased working capital during growth, and potential decline-related costs such as inventory clearance.

Incorporating an understanding of product life cycles into a business plan is indispensable for strategic planning and long-term success. A comprehensive appreciation of the stages allows businesses to proactively manage resources, adapt to changing market conditions, and make informed decisions that drive sustained profitability. As businesses navigate the dynamic landscapes of their products, leveraging the insights provided by product life cycles becomes a cornerstone of effective business planning.

Appendix B: Pain Points

In the context of business, a "pain point" refers to a specific problem, challenge, or frustration that potential customers are experiencing and that a business aims to address. Identifying and understanding these pain points is crucial for businesses to tailor their products, services, or solutions to meet the needs and alleviate the challenges faced by their target audience.

Here are key aspects related to pain points in business:

Customer Challenges: Pain points represent the difficulties or obstacles that customers encounter in their daily lives or business operations. These challenges can range from inefficiencies and inconveniences to more significant problems that hinder their progress or success.

Opportunity for Solutions: Pain points create opportunities for businesses to offer solutions. By addressing these challenges, businesses can provide value to their customers and differentiate themselves from competitors. The ability to effectively resolve pain points contributes to customer satisfaction and loyalty.

Market Research and Understanding: Identifying pain points requires thorough market research and a deep understanding of the target audience. Businesses need to listen to customer feedback, conduct surveys, analyze industry trends, and stay attuned to the evolving needs of their market.

Communication and Marketing: Once pain points are identified, businesses can tailor their communication and marketing strategies to highlight how their products or services specifically address and alleviate these challenges. Clear messaging that resonates with the target audience's pain points can be a compelling way to attract customers.

Product Development: Pain points often drive product or service development. Businesses may innovate to create solutions that directly target and resolve the identified challenges faced by their customers. This iterative process can lead to the creation of products that precisely meet market demands.

Competitive Advantage: Understanding and effectively addressing pain points can be a source of competitive advantage. Businesses that excel in identifying and resolving customer challenges are better positioned to capture market share and build lasting relationships with their clientele.

Personalization: Recognizing individual pain points within a diverse customer base allows for personalized approaches. Businesses can tailor their offerings or services to cater to specific needs, creating a more personalized and relevant customer experience.

Feedback Loops: Establishing feedback loops with customers is crucial for ongoing success. Regularly seeking input from customers helps businesses stay attuned to evolving pain points and ensures that their solutions remain effective and aligned with customer needs.

Examples of pain points in various industries might include:

E-commerce: Complicated checkout processes, high shipping costs, or concerns about the security of online transactions.

Healthcare: Long waiting times, difficulty accessing medical records, or lack of transparent pricing for medical services.

Technology: Incompatibility issues, frequent software crashes, or challenges in integrating different technological solutions.

Finance: Cumbersome loan application processes, hidden fees, or a lack of transparency in financial transactions.

By identifying and addressing pain points effectively, businesses can establish a meaningful connection with their customers, build trust, and create sustainable relationships that contribute to long-term success.

Appendix C: Business Plan Template

Use the template below to outline and create your business plan.

NAME OF ORGANIZATION
ADDRESS
CONTACT INFORMATION
NAME OF AUTHOR

Executive Summary

Use this section to summarize your business and encourage your audience to read further

Industry Overview

In this section, write a summary of the industry in your market segment(s). Explain why your proposed business stands out from the others in the market segment.

Products or Services Offered

Detail your products or services here, focusing on why your customers should choose you over all your competitors.

Market Analysis

Provide a detailed description of the market for your proposed products and services. Focus on your venture's strengths in your market segment.

Marketing and Sales Strategy

Detail your organization's sales and marketing strategy in this section, explaining why your strategy is better than that of your competitors.

Organizational Structure

This is the place to inform your readers of how your business is organized, using organizational flow charts if necessary.

Operations Plan

Include a detailed description of how your business operates here.

Financial Plan

Use this section to outline and enumerate all of the financial operations of your organization. This section is crucial to attracting lenders and investors.

Risk Analysis

List any risks here. Include a detailed risk mitigation strategy for all foreseeable risks involved with your venture.

Implementation Timeline
Detail the steps to implement your vision for your business venture in this section. Include a timeline based on verifiable data and explain all assumptions made for the implementation of various phases of your strategy.

Monitoring and Evaluation
In this section, discuss all the metrics used for monitoring and evaluation of the implementation of of your business strategy.

Supporting Documents (Resumes, Letters of Support, etc.)
Include documentation such as P & L statements, spreadsheets, etc. in this section.

Additional Financial Information
This could include bank statements, or financial information not discussed elsewhere in your business plan.

Legal Documents (Contracts, Agreements, etc.)
This section includes business licenses, contracts, or any legal documents pertaining to your business.

Appendices
This section includes any supporting documents or information not included elsewhere in your business plan.

ABOUT THE AUTHOR

Charlton Hall, PhD has been advising businesses for over forty years. He has run many successful business and is now the Executive Director of Objective Academy, an online organization dedicated to providing continuing education for the real world. You can find more information at www.objectiveacademy.com.

www.ingramcontent.com/pod-product-compliance
Lightning Source LLC
Chambersburg PA
CBHW070931260726
48661CB00003B/929